Twayne's English Authors Series

Sylvia E. Bowman, *Editor*

INDIANA UNIVERSITY

George Saintsbury

(TEAS) 56

George Saintsbury

By WALTER LEUBA

Twayne Publishers, Inc.   ::   New York

Preface

MY object in this volume is a simple one: to give as much indication as possible, George Saintsbury himself participating throughout, of the subject's qualities as critic, essayist, and historian of literature, and of the varied and contradictory reputation which these qualities acquired in the course of a long lifetime and thereafter. Were this the latest of many books on Saintsbury, a generous use of quotation might be questionable. Since it is the first, I have thought it appropriate to allow Saintsbury to speak for himself as much as possible, and also to give due hearing to those who undervalued as well as to those who valued his extraordinary accomplishment.

One of Saintsbury's own critical dicta was that "general opinion of a man is during his lifetime often wrong, for some time after his death almost always so: and the absolute balance is very seldom reached till a full generation—something more than the conventional thirty years—has passed." The thirty years have been accounted for, and it is doubtful if there is yet anything like general agreement as to his stature as critic and historian; but his books continue to be referred to and he is occasionally read. Any reader of this book will wish to consult the brief but very detailed *Biographical Memoir* by Saintsbury's friend and colleague at Edinburgh, A. Blyth Webster. Its forty-two pages are a masterpiece of condensed review.

In this first critical study of any length, I propose to omit even mention of much that Webster considered in order to concentrate attention on Saintsbury's major works and to deal as fully as possible with the reputation he earned, particularly in relation to his "style" and to the critical principles which he observed.

I trust that what follows will provide support for the view that in descriptive historical criticism of the characteristically English kind, now somewhat out of fashion, Saintsbury has no equal in both quality and comprehensiveness. Whether descriptive criticism is, as I believe, both the more valid and the more valuable kind, is not a question here.

WALTER LEUBA

I wish to thank Mr. Edmund Wilson for permission to quote his comments on Saintsbury. Acknowledgment is due also to the many publishers of Saintsbury's work in Great Britain and the United States, particularly to Macmillan & Co., Ltd.; J. M. Dent & Sons, Ltd.; W. Blackwood & Sons; and Oxford University Press.

I owe much to my friend Ernest N. Dilworth of Lehigh University, who read the manuscript; to Evelyn Ristanovich and Hazel Nelson, who typed for me; and to Alexander Ristanovich and my wife who proofread the manuscript.

Contents

Chronology

1845   George Edward Bateman Saintsbury born October 23 at Southampton, the second son of George Saintsbury and Elizabeth Wright. His father is general secretary and superintendent of the docks at Southampton.

1850   The family leaves Southampton for London. Saintsbury attends a dame-school in Norfolk Terrace and later, for five years, King's College School, London, under Dr. Major.

1863   In October, elected to a Second Classical Postmastership, which ran for five years, at Merton College, Oxford.

1868   Receives his B.A. from Oxford; begins eight years of schoolmastering, meanwhile reading, writing, and publishing his first articles and essays. On leaving Oxford, accepts an appointment as teacher of English and history in the Upper Forms of Manchester Grammar School; but his stay in Manchester is brief, from January to July only. Marries Emily Fenn, daughter of Mr. Henry William King, surgeon. In the autumn, begins six years as Classical Master of Elizabeth College on the island of Guernsey; reads French literature extensively.

1873   Begins reviewing for the *Academy*, French and English literature and batches of novels.

1874   Leaves Guernsey and becomes Headmaster at the Elgin Educational Institute at Elgin in Morayshire.

1876   In the autumn, leaves Elgin and settles in London for almost twenty years of journalism and literary activity. He and his family live in London itself for about ten years; from 1887 to 1891 at Fulbourn in Cambridgeshire; and after 1891 in Reading. He begins twelve years of writing for the *St. James Gazette* under Frederick Greenwood.

1877   Has a second brief stay in Manchester, on the staff of the *Manchester Guardian* under C. P. Scott. On his return to London, writes political leaders for the Tory weekly *London* under the editorship of W. E. Henley.

1879   Beginning with the ninth volume of the ninth edition of the *Encyclopaedia Britannica* published this year, contributes thirty-six articles, including the survey of French literature and most of the articles on French authors.

1880   Joins the staff of the *Saturday Review* under Philip Harwood, where he remains until 1894; meanwhile, in 1883, becomes assistant editor under Walter Pollock, Harwood's successor. His first book, *A Primer of French Literature*, is published by The Clarendon Press, Oxford.

1895   In mid-September, appointed by Lord Balfour of Burleigh, secretary for Scotland, to the Regius Chair of English Literature at Edinburgh University as Professor of Rhetoric and English Literature, to succeed David Masson. The three chief candidates were W. E. Henley, Walter Raleigh, and Saintsbury. On October 15 Saintsbury gives his inaugural address.

1898   Receives an Honorary LL.D. at Aberdeen.

1900   The first volume of the *History of Criticism and Literary Taste in Europe* published.

1906   The first volume of the *History of English Prosody* published. Receives an Honorary Litt.D. at Durham.

1909   Becomes president of the English Association and an Honorary Fellow of Merton College, Oxford.

1911   Becomes a Fellow of the British Academy and on October 30, 1912 reads to the academy his Warton Lecture on "The Historical Character of English Lyric."

1912   His *History of English Prose Rhythm* published. Receives an Honorary Litt.D. from Oxford.

1915   After twenty years at Edinburgh, resigns in June and retires. Has to sell his library of some fifteen thousand books. Goes to his native Southampton for a year and then to Bath, where he spends his remaining days.

1916   *The Peace of the Augustans* published.

1917   The first volume of the *History of the French Novel* published.

1919   Receives an Honorary LL.D. from Edinburgh.

1922   In this and the succeeding two years his three *Scrap Books* are published. His elder son, Lewis, dies; the younger,

Christopher, survives his father. On October 23, Saintsbury's seventy-seventh birthday, George Crystal and John C. Squire go to Bath to present him with an address signed by hundreds of his former students and living admirers.

1924 His wife dies, after many years as an invalid.

1925 His portrait is painted by William Nicholson and given by Saintsbury to Merton College, Oxford, where it hangs in the Common Room.

1933 He dies at Bath, January 28, at the age of eighty-seven. His body is taken to Southampton for burial in the Old Cemetery.

CHAPTER 1

The Beginnings

I. Oxford

A S A young man Saintsbury was, he says, "shy and ungregari-
ous"; he was also sensitive, imaginative, critical, and a
voracious reader. He wrote verse and other literary exercises
like most well-nurtured young men, knew they were nothing
more than competent, and later destroyed them. Little is now
known of his childhood beyond his schooling and residences.
"I was born," he wrote of his birthplace in Southampton, "in
one of those houses, not infrequent in the earlier nineteenth
century, which had the name 'Lottery Hall,' because they had
been built out of winnings under that system of public lotteries
which our more intelligent and less canting forefathers permitted
and utilised."[1]

Of the London residences, beginning in his fifth year, he said:
"Midway between Westbourne Grove and Notting Hill Gate lay
one of the new, but not newest, patches of houses, called Pem-
bridge Villas. We lived, on coming from Southampton, first on
the eastern or London side of this, and then, after an intervening
sojourn in the neighbouring Chepstow Place, on the western or
Notting Hill side, where my father first lived and then bought a
house."[2]

His Oxford years, however, are the subject of a series of
extremely reticent reminiscences which he wrote in his late seventies; from them, most of the little information about him is derived.[3] In October, 1864, he entered Merton, "the most sociable
of colleges," under Warden Marsham, "that very perfect speci-
men of one of the best kinds of College 'Heads'." His tutors were
William Sidgwick, Edward Caird, and, in scholarship, John King.
There were forty undergraduates in the college, and among his
friends he soon numbered Mandell Creighton, Robert Raikes,

Stafford Northcote, Mowbray Morris, Forster Alleyne, W. H. Foster, and William Minto.

No one, probably, ever had a keener relish for college life, from the mathematics at which he was *good* to the college cook, Mr. Betteris, whose specialties were hare soup and dressed crab and who is delightfully celebrated in one of the reminiscences referred to above. It would be pointless to paraphrase Saintsbury's varied and numerous allusions to things, events, and persons of these years; for what revelations there are, are more in the manner of the telling than in the facts. He made a little money tutoring in logic. He slept in the light of the moon for two years. He kept a diary and was addicted to waltzing. He and his intimate friends became known as the "Merton Popes" because they observed the fast days. He was a member of the Whist Club. He disliked Aristotle's *Ethics* and rejoiced in the *Politics*. And he took a fancy to scholasticism.

His income at Oxford was under two hundred pounds a year, more than half of which was provided by his family; thus he got into what he calls unjustifiable debt. He bought specially made white gloves for a young lady. He also bought a pair of handsome dueling pistols for five guineas, which he used for shooting at packing-cases and later had to sell for thirty shillings. Poor vision, from which he suffered all his life, made him unsatisfactory at billiards. A "malformation of the hand" made his handwriting "an astonishment and a hissing and a curse to all mankind." He walked twenty-five to thirty miles a day, a mile once in twelve-and-a-half minutes, and forty-three miles in one day: "My one really athletic gift and pleasure was walking." It was not until he was past forty that walking was restricted as the result of a slip on wet asphalt and of a mistreated broken bone above the ankle. He played chess but, like his father, he could not keep his temper at it. He was good at whist, piquet, and loo.

In his second year he met and quickly became intimate with Mandell Creighton, later Bishop Creighton, two years his senior and the author of the standard modern *History of the Papacy*. Creighton was a first-rate *raconteur* and "my Right Reverend, well-beloved, and infinitely respected friend." He and Saintsbury lodged together during the October term of 1866 and had "night long arguments." Creighton was soon to get a fellowship, however, and Saintsbury was left to himself. In Mrs. Creighton's life of her husband there are a few independent references to these years. "One of Creighton's closest friends," Louise Creighton wrote, "was George Saintsbury, . . . known to all his undergraduate friends as 'The Saint.'" She recorded that he and Creighton were the only Merton men reading for honors in "Greats"; that together they took essays to Jowett and attended W. W. Shirley's and Jowett's lectures; and that they were fond of reading in each other's rooms "as well as of sitting up talking till the small hours of the morning," reading aloud, among other things, St. Augustine's *Confessions*. "This proceeding," she added, "was not altogether popular in College."[4]

Creighton had the "amiable knack" of organizing expeditions. Saintsbury wrote to Louise Creighton after her husband's death: "I remember one Trinity Sunday, 1865, when he and I and two men drove to Witney, went to church there, then walked for 20 miles or so through Wychwood, dined late at the Marlborough Arms, and drove back to Oxford just in time for twelve o'clock, on one of the most glorious summer nights I ever remember."[5] An account of another expedition of the kind Saintsbury relished all his life is found in a letter from Creighton, dated "Fifth Sunday in Lent, 1865," to his friend Raikes:

I got up at 8:30 and breakfasted with Saintsbury, and afterwards he and I went off to the Church of SS. Philip and James. I had never been to service before, and I liked it immensely. I never saw an altar I liked so much, or where the effect was so good. Afterwards we discovered Potter and Everest among the congregation, so we joined them unto us and went all in a body for a walk to Wolvercot and Wytham, and lunched at Godstow; and it was such a jolly morning, and we had old Saintsbury on the fuss about things in general. One of his observations was very great: he said that when he was a parson he would strictly adhere to the Canon, and report to the Bishop all his parishioners who did not fast on Fridays, and would prosecute his village butcher in the Court of Arches for selling meat on that day. We then went to Evensong at St. Thomas's at three o'clock, and were the entire congregation except Prothero and the Sunday school girls, who were catechised by Mr. Chamberlain in a lugubrious manner, during which time I refreshed my memory on points of doctrine by perusing the XXXIX Articles, Everest went to sleep, Saintsbury contemplated a picture of the Virgin which he carries about in his Prayer

Book, and Potter blinked dismally and thoughtfully through his eye-glass.[6]

Mrs. Creighton quotes Edward Copleston as saying of her husband: "He was full of Carlyle; he and Saintsbury talked about the 'immensities' and the 'everlasting no,' and divided us all into those who were 'in contact' and those who were not 'in contact' with the great Heart of the Universe."[7] Besides Carlyle, they were "full of" Browning and Tennyson, Morris and Swinburne. Saintsbury brought to Oxford three copies of Swinburne's *Poems and Ballads* as soon as it appeared. He gave one to Creighton "who proceeded at once to read them aloud lying in a hammock in a friend's room from lunch to chapel, and went on again after dinner, till some one pulled away the book and took his turn at reading."

Some comments Saintsbury made in his seventy-seventh year are relevant to this reference to Carlyle. In describing his own opinions as "home-grown, in respect not only of minor 'books and things and persons,' but of the greater matters in politics and religion, in aesthetics and philosophy," Saintsbury adds: "I do not take to myself the slightest credit for this independence. I suppose I was born so, just as another man might be born handsome, a third physically strong, a fourth amiable, and a fifth able to write so that other people can read his writing. At any rate no person that I can think of, in racking a pretty good memory, ever did influence my opinions in the slightest degree, and no author except Carlyle, with whom in details I disagree as often as I agree, if not oftener."[8]

The outcome of these years at Oxford was something Saintsbury could never forget, and it had perhaps more to do with the course of his life than did anything else in his experience. He got a second in "Greats." In old age he wondered "if there is anything, not involving severe bodily pain, utter financial ruin, real disgrace, or the death of a dear friend, which *hurts* so abominably and lasts so long as getting a Second?" "The sting of a Second is almost incurable," he added; and he confessed that he had "recurrent dreams for many years" about it. There were various possible reasons for his failure to get a First: his partiality for Aristotle's *Politics* and his aversion to the *Ethics*; his rebellion, along with Creighton, against the then predominant influence in Oxford of John Stuart Mill; and "his inordinate discursive readings 'out of bounds,'" without which he would not have been George Saintsbury. The night of the day of his humiliation he had what he called a "consolatory" dinner with Robert Raikes.

Saintsbury stood five times for a fellowship, at Wadham, Lincoln, Corpus, and twice at Merton, each time unsuccessfully. He became a member of the Inner Temple, and was engaged to be married. On his last day at Oxford, early in 1868, he got an appointment to teach at Manchester, where he stayed only briefly; and he got married. "If it were possible," he said much later, "and somebody offered me twenty thousand pounds *not* to have gone to Oxford, I would say, 'Thy money perish with thee.'"

II Teaching and Journalism

It was to be many years before Saintsbury was financially comfortable. His terms at Oxford required considerable thrift in spite of his confessed small extravagances. Manchester, although he enjoyed his stay there, did nothing to improve his circumstances. Since he was now married, he looked elsewhere: "It was through the recommendation of Dr. Magrath, then Fellow and afterwards . . . Provost [of Queen's College], that I went to his native Guernsey, and abode there, as in an Island of the Blest, six years, teaching the classics and other things to decently bred youth for hours at which even a trade-union leader could hardly grumble; enjoying the bounties of King Bacchus and my Lady Venus (as Prior Aymer saith); walking, whisting, waltzing; reading immense quantities of French and other literature; writing my first reviews for the *Academy* on Théodore de Banville and the Goncourts; 'regarding the ocean' like my august neighbor and fellow-*incola*, M. Victor Hugo—in short, possessing almost all desirable possessions save one—to wit, money."

Saintsbury also did outside lecturing and private coaching. Although Hugo was a neighbor on the island, as Thackeray had earlier been in Kensington, Saintsbury never met either.

After the six years at Guernsey he went to Scotland in a financially unsuccessful experiment as headmaster of a grammar school, the Elgin Educational Institute in Morayshire. Of this episode he recorded that he lost "about a third of my scanty patrimony" trying to "start a kind of grammar-school on something like English lines, in the north of Scotland," and he added that "it was in Elgin that I made my first separate study of a great English writer—Dryden; in Elgin that I began to read Elizabethan literature more than sporadically."[10] Two years later, in 1876, he gave up schoolmastering, settled in London, and began his career as an active journalist. He saw much of his friends, including Andrew Lang and Austin Dobson. Edmund Gosse wrote on July 24, 1877, of having been in Saintsbury's company with Lang and Dobson and of having found him very interesting "but a little feverish and perfervid." He described him as "the electric Saintsbury."[11] Roger Lancelyn Green in his biography of Lang, noted that "Saintsbury was probably Lang's most intimate friend between about 1875 and 1885, when they were accustomed to walk home together from the City to Kensington three or four days a week."[12]

After his mother's death in 1877, the receipt of a small inheritance made it possible for Saintsbury to clear himself of debts, some of which dated from Oxford, and to furnish a small house for his family. Meanwhile, however, still at Elgin, he began his ten-year association with the *Fortnightly Review,* after John Morley, the editor, accepted for publication his esssay on Baudelaire. "I had found schoolmastering . . . not only not at all dear to me," he said, punning, "but exceedingly expensive," and he "fled" to the Press "for refuge."[13] He later added: "I own that I never liked schoolmastering: and though both Guernsey and Elgin provided excellent 'condolences,' I was horribly hard up all the time."[14]

With the Baudelaire essay, a daring subject in the England of that time, Saintsbury was launched on his critical, if not his journalistic, career.[15] It was the first in any way adequate consideration of the poet in English, and there had been little in French itself. It exemplified Saintsbury's critical qualities at once: independence of judgment, proportion, and strict relevance of treatment. Writing in 1933 after Saintsbury's death, A. Blyth

Webster asked: "How many critics have made as sound a start, or one that wears as well after all but sixty years?"[16]

Once in London, journalism proved a genuine "refuge" and his circumstances improved rapidly. And from this point on, despite his ever-increasing journalistic and editorial duties, considered essays on both French and English writers continued to appear in the *Fortnightly Review*, in *Macmillan's Magazine*, in *Merry England*, in *The National Review*, in *The Saturday Review*, and in *The New Review*, and elsewhere. These essays were collected, with a few additions, as books and published: two series of *Essays in English Literature*, one in 1890 and the second in 1895; *Essays on French Novelists* in 1891; and *Miscellaneous Essays* in 1892. These, with additional material, were again republished in the four volumes of the *Collected Essays and Papers* of 1923-24.

Saintsbury's essays as represented in these collections were and remain unexcelled as both criticism and literature. Despite his own disclaimer that *fine writing* was not his trade,[17] they have rarely been equaled since. They are shorter than the early nineteenth-century "essay" that appeared regularly in the *Edinburgh* and in other reviews; and they do not have the common tendency of many of those essays to show off the critic's superior, specialized knowledge of the subjects dealt with by the writer being reviewed. Saintsbury criticized literature *as* literature, and his comments on subject matter are informative and descriptive. Only his enjoyment is subjective. Saintsbury's essays are, certainly, by now a familiar type: the literary discourse on a writer and his work, on "the man and his books." Yet few critics have managed such discussions so well, so reliably, and so effectively. He tells just enough about the author to establish him as a human figure in time and place, and he does so with none of the atmosphere of the handbook or biographical dictionary, and without small talk and gossip. Then he discourses on the work, on the books themselves, not as a theorist nor as a man with an axe to grind, but as the informed reader recommending to the next reader what has already recommended itself to him.

The essays engage and hold our interest; and they send us, as few essays do and as Saintsbury always, throughout his life, intended that they should, to the books themselves. That he refuses in general to make up our minds for us, gives us no "position" to take with respect to a writer, but instead invites us to find out for ourselves, has been held against him. He has no "theory" of literature, does not want one, and has only a casual interest in the theories of others. As a notorious Tory, he praises the work of "radicals." He takes no moral, ethical, political, or social position as a critic; and, consequently, those who look to criticism mainly for something other than literature itself do not know where to place Saintsbury.

Saintsbury's essays in English literature cover the period from 1780 to 1860 and are, in many instances, the first considered treatments of their subjects, which range from James Hogg, Sydney Smith, J. G. Lockhart, and George Borrow, to political satire, the historical novel, and criticism itself. The miscellaneous volume of 1892 deals with both French and English writers and subjects, including the remarkable preface on "English Prose Style" (from the *Specimens of English Prose Style from Malory to Macaulay* which he had selected and annotated in 1885), and another essay on "Modern English Prose," dating from 1876. The essays on French novelists include twelve studies ranging from Anthony Hamilton and Lesage to Flaubert and Murger.

The essays established him as an unusual critic—unusual, then and since—in that he stuck to his subject and to the business at hand. As we have noted, he did not use criticism for the indulgence of eccentricities, gossip, or theory. Since the essays were also found extremely useful by the increasing numbers of writers, lecturers, and teachers (general and specialized) who were dealing with literature and literary figures, Saintsbury became more and more widely known as an authority, particularly on English and French literature. He was constantly quoted, deferred to, and taken issue with. One result of this general recognition was that he was offered work of all kinds, of which he accepted only as much as suited him. In the field of literature he did no hack work and nothing that was distasteful to him.

Most of this work dates from the period when Saintsbury made his living as a political journalist and editor. His output, the larger part of it never republished, was enormous. As for what did reach book form, the beginnings of the series of literary histories will be dealt with later: three of them appeared between 1880 and 1887. His study of Dryden for the English Men of Letters Series appeared in 1881; an annotated selection of French lyrics in 1882; *Marlborough,* in the English Worthies Series, in 1885; *Manchester,* in the Historic Towns Series, in 1887; translations of Balzac's *The Chouans,* of Mérimée's *Chronicles of the Reign of Charles IX,* and of Edmond Scherer's *Essays on English Literature* were published in 1890 and 1891. There were also dozens of other things: editings of six French texts for the Clarendon Press and of one for the Cambridge Pitt Press Series, prefaces and introductions to English and French classics far too numerous to mention; and editions of the complete works of Fielding, Herrick, and Sterne. Saintsbury also contributed thirty-six articles on French writers to the ninth edition of the *Encyclopaedia Britannica* (revising these and adding two more to the eleventh edition in 1910-11). He wrote eight articles for *Chambers' Encyclopaedia* and thirteen for H. D. Traill's *Social England.*

And there was much more. Saintsbury had an unusual flair for writing prefaces and introductions of the kind that not only can be read with pleasure before reading the text that follows, but invite an even more delightful rereading afterward. Preface writing tends either to be dull, fulfilling an apparently necessary conventional function: to underline the obvious and to give away some of the surprise of the text, or to venture perverse views and irrelevancies. Saintsbury early discovered an approach to the problem that avoided all these pitfalls and provided instead the precise foretaste to suit the occasion. He was neither pretentious nor over-instructive, and he was never solemn. He simply beckoned the reader to enjoyment. Well over a hundred volumes contain his beguilements, some brief, some extensive; but most of them are the very best of their kind.

III The Historian of Literature

Saintsbury began his remarkable series of "histories" with a modest *Primer of French Literature,* published in the Clarendon

Press Series in 1880. A book strictly for beginners, it was, in fact, an essay of one hundred forty pages which he referred to, in the preface to the second edition when at the request of friends he added an index, as "little more than an index in itself."[18] Andrew Lang had read the proofs. Succeeding editions were revised, corrected, and extended; and the work was kept in print for half a century.

Brief as it is, it has none of the patronizing, over-simplified, and secondhand nature of the typical primer. To use it requires, and rewards, intelligence; and, summary as the dealings with individual authors and periods are of necessity, the presentation is full of life. Following a description of the Chansons de Gestes, for example, Saintsbury continues: "Not quite so early as these poems, but soon afterwards, there began to be written another kind of romance," and to *romance* he provides a footnote: "It should be observed that this word indicates the character and popularity of early French literature. *Enromancer* properly means 'to turn into French.' "[19] The primer admirably supplies that "mind-map of the general subject" which he desiderated many years later in the preface to that other excellent primer produced in 1914, *A First Book of English Literature.*[20]

In 1882 Saintsbury followed up the French primer with an extraordinary full-length treatment of the subject to which the primer had been "an introduction." *A Short History of French Literature* he defined as "an attempt to present to students a succinct history of the course of French literature compiled from an examination of that literature itself. . . ."[21] He then announced one of the principles to which he adhered faithfully in all of his historical and critical writing, a principle which accounts in part at least for both the validity of his judgments and the continuous freshness of his presentation: "Manuscript sources I do not pretend to have consulted; but any judgment which is passed in this book may be taken as founded on personal acquaintance with the book or author unless the contrary is stated. Some familiarity with the subject has convinced me that nowhere are opinions of doubtful accuracy more frequently adopted and handed on without inquiry than in the history of literature."[22]

The book, like its predecessor, was kept in print for many

editions for which Saintsbury supplied corrections, deletions, additions, and rewordings. It was, and continued to be, well received in England. In France, Paul Bourget gave it high praise; and the medieval chapters were approved by no less an authority than Gaston Paris.[23] In 1887, however, Edmond Scherer attempted to discredit the book as showing characteristically English superficiality. He went so far as to accuse Saintsbury of writing about books he had not read, a charge impossible to support though it must have seemed to Scherer (though it did not to Gaston Paris) beyond reason that an Englishman could have read the number of French works assessed in the *Short History.*[24] Saintsbury recognized Scherer's strictures in his preface to the third edition (1889); and he had the last word on the subject when, in 1891, after Scherer's death, he selected, translated, prefaced, and courteously and appreciatively introduced a volume of Scherer's own essays on English writers.[25] As an estimate of Saintsbury's work in French literature, we cite the judgment of Huntington Cairns.

"As a systematic expositor of French literature to the English public," wrote Cairns in his introduction to *French Literature and Its Masters,* "Saintsbury was without a peer. . . . In his general histories . . . his inclusive treatment and wonderful powers of organization left him without a rival."[26]

Saintsbury continued his series of histories with *A History of Elizabethan Literature,* the first of its kind, in 1887. Its 461 pages covered a hundred-year period beginning in 1560, and in the preface he again stated his methods: "I have never (unless in some very rare case specially indicated), delivered on any author mentioned a judgment based on second-hand information. . . ." And he adds:

I will warrant every critical judgment and description, general and particular, in the following pages to be, unless the contrary is stated, based on original reading and thought. My dates and my biographical facts I take for the most part from others; and though I shall be glad (after verification) to make any correction, I shall not feel deeply convinced of sin if it turns out that I have dated this poet's *Tears of Melancholy* in March 1593, when the true date is May 1595; or asserted that that poet's grandmother was Joan Smith, who is buried at Little Peddlington, instead of Jane Smith, who was married at Kennaquhair. These things, interesting perhaps and sometimes valuable in their own way, are but ancillary, if even that, to the history of literature in the proper and strict sense; and it is the history of literature in the proper and strict sense with which I have to deal.[27]

Saintsbury has had competitors but no equals in the kind of strictly literary history he undertook, and his stated and variously restated methods and principles are largely responsible for the liveliness and reliability of his judgments.

The Elizabethan volume was planned by the publisher, Macmillan, as one of four volumes covering all of English literature, each by a different writer. It was the first of the four to appear, and eventually Saintsbury took over the modern volume, originally in the hands of Edward Dowden. This work, which appeared in 1896 as *A History of Nineteenth Century Literature (1780-1895)*,[28] followed a plan similar to the Elizabethan volume except that he touched on the question of dealing with living authors and decided not to discuss them though he made an almost necessary exception of Ruskin. Saintsbury was later to elaborate, as will be noted elsewhere, on the reasons, apart from his strictly journalistic activity as a reviewer, that he thought it unwise to deal with contemporary writers, whether as a historian or as a university lecturer.

In the preface he stated another of his critical principles: "I have attempted to preserve a perfectly independent and, as far as possible, a rationally uniform judgment, taking account of none but literary characteristics, but taking account of all characteristics that are literary."[29] And he proceeded to recognize the difficulty of preserving this "achromatic" view of literature, as he called it, as literature itself approaches the contemporary period. Most readers realize the strong control that natural prejudice, personal knowledge of the writer, current fashion, and other temporary circumstances exercise over tastes and preferences among contemporaries.

The final volume in this series of what might be called preliminary histories was *A Short History of English Literature*, published in 1898; but it had been undertaken four years earlier before the appointment to Edinburgh. In the preface Saintsbury explained that his object

is to give, from the literary point of view only, and from direct reading of the literature itself, as full, as well supplied, and as conveniently
arranged a storehouse of facts as the writer could provide. The substitution of bird's-eye views and sweeping generalisations for positive
knowledge has been very sedulously avoided; but it is hoped that the
system of Interchapters will provide a sufficient chain of historical
summary as to general points, such as, for instance, the nature and
progress of English prosody and the periods of prose style.[30]

This "short" history is the longest of them, 797 pages on its
first appearance; in fact, David Nichol Smith considered it
"among his [Saintsbury's] big books" and added that "in view
of the extent of ground which it covers, the freshness and the
confidence of its judgments, and the remarkably short time in
which it was written—less I believe than a year—I am inclined
to consider [it] his greatest *tour de force.*"[31]

The attacks on Saintsbury's competence were few but notorious; and they cannot be overlooked in a study of his work,
though here they must be handled briefly. The first and most
famous of these was occasioned by the present *Short History*,
and the man who made the attack was John Churton Collins.
Many years before, in 1881, Saintsbury had said among other
acknowledgments in his English Men of Letters *Dryden*: "To
Mr. J. Churton Collins I owe thanks for pointing out to me a
Dryden house which, so far as he and I know, has escaped the
notice of previous biographers."[32] Collins' slating appeared in
the *Saturday Review;* what prompted his virulence against this
"masterpiece of its kind," which is still in print after sixty-five
years, is not known. A. Blyth Webster, who provided the most
succinct and best comment on the review which Collins later
included in an appropriately titled volume, *Ephemera Critica,*[33]
noted that Collins accused Saintsbury of

"scandalous" "almost incredible" errors; of "random" and "audacious"
assertions; of ignorance "astounding" and "of the very rudiments"; of
commenting on works which he "could not even have inspected" (the
old discourtesy and uncharity, never less in court); of criticism "almost
uniformly as absurd in what it praises as in what it censures"; of
"vulgarity, coarseness, grossness," and "boisterous pride" in these.
Brave words. . . . In such straits it seems we are not left to ourselves.
There is an Irony that watches over us. There were almost as many

mistakes in the offensive article as in the offending book. Of some fifty errors alleged, some seven stood their ground, and were silently, but not in haste, corrected. The alterations amount to five dates, one proper name, and one amended sentence.[34]

One bitter reproach serves as an example since it amused Saintsbury to remember it in print on several later occasions. "On page 482," Collins said, "John Pomfret, the author of one of the most popular poems of the eighteenth century, is called Thomas."[35] Much of Saintsbury's character is suggested by the footnote on this in the second volume of the *History of Criticism*: "Let me draw special attention to 'John.' I once, unwittingly or carelessly, called him 'Thomas,' and I am afraid that I even neglected to correct the error in a second edition of the guilty book. A man who writes 'Thomas' for 'John,' in the case of a minor poet, can, I am aware, possess no virtues, and must expect no pardon. But I shall always henceforth remember to call him 'Pomfret, Mr. *John*.' 'Let this expiate,' as was remarked in another case of perhaps not less mortal sin."[36] But Saintsbury had actually been there beforehand. In the preface to the *Short History* he had clearly said: "None but a charlatan will pretend that he has himself written, and none but a very unreasonable person will expect anyone else to write, a history of the kind free from blunders."[37]

Saintsbury was now prepared for the writing of his major works; following his appointment to Edinburgh, they began to appear. His critical principles and methods, restated in various forms throughout his active life, were already established on a solid basis. He was critic, historian, and writer; a scholar also, though not in the modern specialized sense nor in the older pedantic one; a polyglot reader, at home in Greek, Latin, French, and German, and no stranger to Italian, Spanish, and Icelandic; and a man whose mind was extraordinarily well stocked in the experiences of life as well as in many literatures. That he lived heartily anyone may discover independently of his larger works; one may accept in this respect the evidence of the *Scrap Books*.

CHAPTER 2

Dissonance and Harmonies

I The Discords of Criticism

SAINTSBURY's four major historical works are, in the order of publication, *A History of Criticism and Literary Taste in Europe from the Earliest Texts to the Present Day*, three volumes; *A History of English Prosody from the Twelfth Century to the Present Day*, three volumes; *A History of English Prose Rhythm*, one volume; and *A History of the French Novel*, two volumes. The first of these works is on the largest scale in both substance and time and is, perhaps, his masterpiece; the second, the most instructive, is a detailed application of the great principles of criticism analyzed in the first; the third is the most controversial; and the fourth, the most entertaining. Together, these books are a unique performance in both volume and quality, in the breadth and clarity of the writer's perspective, in the vast range of firsthand experience of the materials dealt with, and in the verve and variety of the presentation. These major works are broadly planned, carefully organized, fully documented, and written in a manner as far from the academic as the writings they discuss. They are written not as projects in research and study, nor as industrious compilations; but, from a full experience of life, they are books to be read and relished. They are intended to stimulate, as much as to satisfy, curiosity; and in no sense do they avoid giving occasion for controversy when such seems fitting to the writer. Saintsbury had sufficient reason to trust his judgment, and his manner made it clear that he did so.

The more than 1,700 pages of the *History of Criticism*, "that epic of literary taste,"[1] or "that encyclopaedic work in which the great critics of the past lie embalmed in academic pedantry,"[2] published between 1900 and 1904 by William Blackwood of

Edinburgh, were the product of Saintsbury's full maturity. Fifty-five in 1900, he had already been professor of rhetoric and English literature for some time; and he also had behind him long years of experience in criticism; in literary and other historical studies; in biography, translation, and editing; in political and other journalism; in reviewing; and in schoolmaster-ing. The work considers historically all those writers who have either expressed formally or informally principles or theories of criticism, or have by their practice of criticism implied principles or theory.

In the preface to Volume I, Saintsbury acknowledged the project to be audacious and described it as "an attempt to supply for others," on the basis of more than thirty years of exploration, "the Atlas of which the writer himself so sorely felt the need."[3] Oliver Elton described it as an "immense chronicle, embracing hundreds of authors famous and obscure, classical, French, Italian, German, and English. . . ."[4] Saintsbury had no predecessor in the field as he defined it; and his definition itself not only is unexceptionable but is of the utmost interest to those who prefer reading to more popular kinds of activity. "The Criticism which will be dealt with here," he says on his opening page, "is the function of the judgment which busies itself with the goodness or badness, the success or ill-success, of literature from the purely literary point of view."

In other words, the Criticism or modified Rhetoric, of which this book attempts to give a history, is pretty much the same thing as the reasoned exercise of Literary Taste—the attempt, by examination of literature, to find out what it is that makes literature pleasant, and therefore good—the discovery, classification, and as far as possible tracing to their sources, of the qualities of poetry and prose, of style and metre, the classification of literary kinds, the examination and "proving," as arms are proved, of literary means and weapons, not neglecting the observation of literary fashions and the like.[5]

And, in the preface to Volume III, he adds:

A friend who is at once friendly, most competent, and of a different complexion in critical thought, objected to me that I "treat literature as something by itself." I hastened to admit the impeachment, and to declare that this is the very postulate of my book. That literature can be *absolutely* isolated is, of course, not to be thought of; nothing human can be absolutely isolated from the general conditions of humanity, and from the other functions and operations thereof. But in that *comparative* isolation and separate presentation which Aristotle meant by his caution against confusion of kinds, I do thoroughly believe.[6]

These ideas and the implied approach to literature are central to Saintsbury's histories and to his writing generally. He was clearly aware of the risks. In the second volume in the final chapter, in which he reviews "The Balance-Sheet of Neo-Classicism," he said that "it is still (1902) the very rarest thing to find a critic who, by equipment or even by inclination, is himself disposed to take a really catholic view of literature; and those who do endeavour to take such a view are constantly regarded with distrust by the general, and with a rather comic rancour by specialists."[7] "In approaching a critic," Elton wrote, "Saintsbury asks what are his working principles, or *media axiomata,* what light they throw on literature, and how literature itself confirms or refutes them."[8] Such is Saintsbury's position; and nothing in his entire work, apart from his manner of writing or "style," has been the source of more objection.

Two formidable critics, both otherwise favorable, must be mentioned. Joel E. Spingarn found Volume II of *History of Criticism* "an important contribution to modern scholarship in the field of critical history." He noted Saintsbury's "impressionistic method and his keen personal prepossessions" and his "aggressively romantic" sympathies. Yet, he added, in the "lack of philosophic unity and co-ordination, and in its neglect of recent research in the same field—it [the work] misses the touch of finality."[9] I would guess that this "touch of finality," whatever it may be in anything but the very highest ranges of verbal expression, is still far to seek. Benedetto Croce discovered Saintsbury to be "equally skilled in literature and innocent of philosophy," and he characterized the three volumes of the *History of Criticism* as "instructive in many ways but [as] wholly deficient in method and definite object." The point is that Saintsbury deliberately excluded any discussion of "metaphysical aesthetic and other manifestations whose interaction and development are the fabric of history itself."[10]

Saintsbury was "innocent of philosophy" only in the sense that George Berkeley was. His mind worked on the data furnished by his senses and on nothing else. As to deficiency in method, it is enough to point out that his methods, clearly described in prefaces and elsewhere, always included, or directed the reader to, the evidence for his assessments. This practice is not always that of theorists. And what Croce meant by "definite object" was known only to himself.

In 1944 Dorothy Richardson was echoing the same or similar complaints. Saintsbury "had an unphilosophic mind."[11] But how do we determine the presence or absence of a philosophic mind, which I take to be something different from being a philosopher, a title Saintsbury never claimed? There is plenty of evidence in his work, certainly, that he had read and comprehended the philosophers from Plato to Nietzsche. There must, therefore, be something more to this term. Miss Richardson was reasonably clear as to what she desiderated in the historian of literature, for she said of Saintsbury that the relationship of literature "to politics, religion, economics, sociology, and so forth, he excluded from his sphere as a historian; as a result he has lost favor and respect as a literary historian."[12] I assume that the presence of these "relativities" in his work makes a writer acceptably philosophic.

What really troubles the experts and the philosophers is Saintsbury's ubiquitous "pleasure principle"—it would seem that the serious intellectual world, then and still, is more puritanical than it knows. What is it that makes literature pleasant, and therefore good? I, too, take it to be the purpose and the whole purpose of the criticism of literature to provide the answer to this question in each specific instance under consideration. To believe this aim in no way minimizes the value—the varied values —of a book. There is doubtless much else besides pleasure to be found in books, even in books that are literature; but, in the long run, nothing matters but the delight they continue to give. If the vitality of delight fades from them, what is left is food for worms, real or analogical.[13]

Volume I of the *History of Criticism* deals with Classical and medieval criticism; Volume II, with the Renaissance "to the decline of eighteenth century orthodoxy"; and Volume III, with

modern criticism; "present day" in the general title is taken to
mean "to 1900." The volumes are broken down into books and
the books into chapters; and the books themselves are followed
by an interchapter in which the writer surveyed and commented
upon general aspects of the material in the preceding book. As
may be deduced, the *History* "was a task of unimaginable difficulty, long neglected and often shirked, on a subject not in
favour, anything but promising, and largely unexplored. It involved Greek, Latin, Italian, French, Spanish, and German as
well as English." As A. Blyth Webster has said, quoting W. P.
Ker: "there are hardly words available to praise the heroism of
the undertaking."[14]

Most readers, those who have read rather than "examined" or
used these volumes, have formulated similar impressions; and
they have also found, as Webster did, that the work "cleared
up large parts of the past, brought light to dark places of literature, and supplied some chapters of the *History of Human
Error*."[15] And it proved, once and for all, Saintsbury's scholarship; however "apt to be cavalier" was his attitude to "ancillaries
and to other aims," his scholarship was far broader and sounder
than could be found elsewhere among his generations of contemporaries. Elton called the work "his widest and lengthiest
contribution to learning" and added that, though it is "indeed,
on the lengthy side" and "has had many critics . . . no one
has tried to do the work again."[16]

In the course of the three volumes Saintsbury considers
chronologically each Classical and European critic of literature
and each theorist of literary criticism. He summarizes and illus-
trates, by paraphrase and quotation, their views, judgments, and
basic position in the history of criticism. These views, judgments,
and theories he assesses historically in the light of the critic's
experiences and times and in the context of their relevance to
the literature from which they were derived, indicating the
"taste" upon which they were founded or which they originated
or encouraged. Each critic's relative contribution to the history
of criticism is appraised, and his work is compared in its validity
and influence with that of his predecessors and contemporaries.
For the first time, a vast body of critical thinking is organized
chronologically, placed in historical perspective, and judged.

The major critics, from Aristotle to Coleridge and beyond, gain by this long historical perspective and by the careful analysis of the many minor figures who preceded, accompanied, or followed them. The result is a panoramic view of Western criticism and taste that is enlivened by copious and diverting allusion and reflection. Primary and secondary sources are carefully documented.

The *History* remains a magnificent one; not, perhaps, in its language, though that is always fresh and idiosyncratic, but certainly in its ordering and presentation of a tremendous amount of detailed information, and in its analysis, comparison, and estimate of this information by an independent, sensitive intelligence. The reading may be "rough going" to some tastes, but anyone who notices the title pages should be aware that he is not embarking on a simple voyage and that the material itself will require serious, though far from deadly serious, attention. A faithful reading of the entire work gives the reader at least one unmatched perspective on what is civilized in Western civilization.

At the request of his publishers, Saintsbury later prepared a revision, adaptation, and supplementation of the English chapters of the *History of Criticism* that was published as a single volume in 1911.[17] Another outgrowth of the larger history was, through the suggestion of Charles Mills Gayley, then of the University of California, the provision for an American publisher of a volume of serviceable extracts in English from the critics themselves.[18] With the exception of those from Aristotle, which Saintsbury adapted from existing translations, all the translations from Classical and foreign authors were his own.

II The Harmony of Verse

In a passage in his *Short History of English Literature*, discussing the work of Henry Hallam, one of his few predecessors in English, Saintsbury remarked "the strange slowness . . . with which English criticism mastered the comparative method" and the consequent limitations of Hallam's literary criticism, particularly in his *Introduction to the Literature of Europe*. And he went on to say: "For Hallam came a little too early to avail

himself of that rediscovery of its earlier treasures which every
nation in Europe made as a consequence of the Romantic movement; he was very partially in sympathy with that movement;
and though he could understand he could not love—a nearly fatal
disqualification for a literary critic or even a literary historian."[19]
The next big work Saintsbury produced, the three volume *History of English Prosody,* is incontrovertible evidence that he
himself had no such disqualification.

The *Prosody* reviews historically the prosodists and the prosodic practice of poets writing in English, relates theory and
practice to the character of English verse, and assesses the comparative contribution of each. Though Saintsbury could not write
a line of poetry himself and knew it, of all literatures it was the
poetry, of which he was "an unsatiated and insatiable lover,"
that enraptured him most; and he had a flawless ear for its
presence in six or more languages. Further, as a critic, he could
account for the operations of poetry on the mind and on the
imagination without in any sense pretending to account for its
creation in the first place.

George N. Shuster's observation that "it is true that the author
of *A History of English Prosody* has a good many blind spots,
that his system of scansion is a bit elementary, and that he can
be willful, careless, and eccentric," is almost a stereotype of the
"qualified" appreciation of Saintsbury's work. Yet Shuster is emi-
nently right despite his vocabulary when he proceeds to say:
"yet it seems to me that nobody else has sensed so well the
marvelous unity of English verse or has been so willing to objec-
tivize his own responses to the beauty of a line or image."[20]

The *History of English Prosody* is, therefore, a brilliant record
of Saintsbury's lifelong delight in the English Muse. His was love
at first sight and love lasting, and nothing if not critical. The
volumes almost burst with life and learning, but the detailed per-
ceptions and discriminations, the analyses of specific phrases,
lines, and passages, the glosses, and the comparative assessments
of each poet's prosodic practice give the *History* its irresistible
interest for every reader to whom poetry is, as it was to Saintsbury, Parnassus itself. Poetry is not for those who can "take it or
leave it," nor has it ever been anything but an uncomfortable subject of instruction or research. Self-important critics and readers

have always been a little ill at ease with Saintsbury's eclecticism
and immediate embrace; they have found in these volumes much
to quibble about, object to, disagree with, and regret. They are
protected from Saintsbury's contagious delight and annoyed by
his oceanic knowledge.

Amy Lowell, an intensely "prosy" poet, faced with the *Prosody*,
illustrated the extreme form of this rejection by describing
Saintsbury as academic and unintelligent. Saintsbury was unduly modest and he would probably have agreed "that there are
many things about poetry which the eminent professor had not
plumbed."[21] Miss Lowell, however, *had* plumbed; and she is
unlikely to return to the surface. But George Sampson briefly
expressed a far more reasonable and typical view in his *Concise
Cambridge History of English Literature.* He called the *Prosody*
"the standard and necessary treatise, delightful to read and delightful even to differ from . . . with its wealth of illustration
and *obiter dicta.*"[22] And it *was* differed from, though chiefly on
the technical side, in the matter of prosodic systems.

The two previous attempts at a history of English prosody
—one by William Mitford in 1774 (much expanded in 1804), and
the other by Edwin Guest in 1836-38—were both generously dealt
with in the *History of English Prosody.* Neither work bears, however, the least resemblance to the book Saintsbury produced.
His purpose was to examine "through at least seven hundred
years of verse, what the prosodic characteristics of English have
actually been, and what goodness or badness of poetry has accompanied the expression of those characteristics." He went on
to say: "I believe I have read nearly all the printed stock of
English verse before 1600; and I know that I have read every
poet of the slightest repute since that date, and a great number
of poets who neither have nor deserve any." And he added in a
footnote: "As these statements are sometimes misunderstood, I
may perhaps be allowed to say that this is not in the least a
boast, but merely a guarantee. That it should be superfluous, I
quite admit: whether it is, I leave those who know to judge."[23]

The book is "a history of prosodic study as well as of prosodic
expression."[24] On the technical subject of prosody, Saintsbury
not only took issue with most of his predecessors, who generally

applied theory to convenient verse rather than derived theory from available verse; but Saintsbury found that a great many of his contemporaries and successors just as emphatically took issue with him. What to me is most curious is that, though the subject of prosody is, as Saintsbury himself acknowledged, a "fair field full of *fighting* folk," there should be so much argumentative interest in the technical aspects of verse and in theories of meter, stress, quantity, etc. Saintsbury, to the annoyance of almost all prosodic specialists, took as usual a common-sense view of the matter: he trusted his ear; and he never forgot that "the Rule comes from the Work, not the Work from the Rule."[25]

There is no mystery to Saintsbury's view; he did not explain the inexplicable: "the central idea" of the book was "that feet or 'spaces' are the integers, the grounds, the secret, of English prosody."[26] And as he proceeded to deal, in 1,548 pages, with the whole of English verse from the Canute Song to Walt Whitman and Robert Bridges, it was the "foot" all the way, with, finally, at the end of the third volume, a solid defense of his findings in a series of appendices, the first of which answered clearly and explicitly the question "What is a Foot?"

Later in the year in which the third volume was published (1910), his *Historical Manual of English Prosody* appeared; a recasting of the three-volume work, it was intended mainly for the university student and for the general reader. In this work, in the second, third, and fourth chapters of Book I, Saintsbury summarily reviewed and provided reasoned analyses of the three main prosodic theories or systems: the accent or stress, the syllabic, and the foot system; and he reaffirmed his conviction that only the foot system could adequately account for English verse.

He returned once again to the subject in his address to the British Academy on May 28, 1919. He acknowledged that, although his *Prosody* and the later *Prose Rhythm* were "received with a good deal of favour, these books, as treatises on one of the most controversial of all subjects could not fail to be, were met with not a little disagreement; and, whether by coincidence or consequence, prosodic studies, which had already been somewhat numerous, have multiplied since; most of them, as was again likely, being based on principles different from, not to say opposed to, mine."[27] He recalled that the prosodic system illustrated by his histories was labeled by one writer "mishmash" and by another "drivel." He then restated his procedure:

My object was not to construct an *a priori* theory of prosody at all, but to examine the prosodic substance of English poetry as a whole, and to discover, if possible, in what way it was constructed. I found, as it seemed to me, and to not a few others, that a system of syllabic equivalence and substitution composing, and equating or contrasting, different prosodic units for which I kept the old traditional name of feet, pervaded the whole of it, from at least the twelfth century onwards, some elements of this being far earlier.[28]

The rest of the address contains his comments on the various increasingly popular systems. He makes it quite clear, as Elton noted, that all inquiries into the physical, or physiological, bases of meter, and all attempts to measure them by machinery, are "*meta*prosodic," outside the field; and all attempts to record prosody in musical terms are vain.[29] This statement Elton gently interpreted as a "refusal to go too far 'behind' the matter in hand." Yet the "matter in hand" was not the "basis of metre" but English prosodic theory and practice.

Even in the *Manual,* however, Saintsbury dealt with the "appreciation of the actual poetry" as the basis for all technical matters; and this approach resulted in the remarkable quality of the larger work. Though one may disagree with Saintsbury's prosodic system, it is still possible to enjoy his *History* of the subject; but to disagree with his view of poetry itself will greatly reduce the amount of possible enjoyment. If the reader disagrees, however, it is probable that poetry is not his preference and that therefore he will have no interest in prosody. I have sometimes thought that even Saintsbury's prose about prose and his prose about food and wine and politics are mainly for lovers of poetry. Be that as it may, Saintsbury opposed all ideas and definitions that tended to place the interest of poetry in the non-poetical, or elsewhere than in the poetry itself. This shift in emphasis was his main objection to Matthew Arnold's famous definition, which he dealt with on a number of occasions. He would have none of it, persistent as it was. His last word on the subject came in old age. "Apropos of Mr. Arnold," he said,

I think the old fallacy-heresy as to Poetry being "a criticism of life" seems to be raising its head again, and it may be well to give it a friendly tap on that head. In one sense all actions, functions, and features of life are "criticisms" of it; taking a constitutional and eating your dinner are tacitly, or tacitly require, such criticisms, with the conclusions that if you do not take exercise you will not live healthily, that if you do not eat you will not live at all. Further, there is of course *in poetry* sublime criticism of life in the ordinary sense, but that criticism does not make the poetry. In other words, some poetry is criticism of life and some criticism of life is poetry; but the restriction in quantification is doubly necessary. And this restriction makes the phrase, as a definition of poetry, or even a general characterisation of it, quite useless, and not improbably misleading.[30]

This statement is, of course, clear enough and explicit enough to provide for endless controversy and disagreement, particularly among those to whom English poetry is a subject rather than an experience. Saintsbury's book is called, and it is, a *History of English Prosody;* but it is also the most encompassing and penetrating kind of history of English poetry itself because of its multitude of representative quotation and because of the comparative prosodic analyses of them. It is regrettable if the word *prosody* in the title holds off any reader, for in these volumes the actual treasures of English verse themselves show forth the prosody; and the theorists who accompany these treasures are for the most part, in the light cast by Saintsbury's wit and enthusiasm, both amusing and instructive.

III The Other Harmony of Prose

Saintsbury had produced, in addition to his professional work at Edinburgh and much miscellaneous editing and prefacing, one volume of a major work every two years since 1900. *A History of English Prose Rhythm* in 1912 was the seventh, and there were three more volumes to come—one on the eighteenth century and two on the French novel. In a note to the preface of the *Prose Rhythm*, Saintsbury emphasized that "this attempts only to be a *History of English Prose Rhythm*, illustrated by examples from writers greater and lesser—not a *History of English Prose Style* generally."[31] And, as in his earlier histories, he disclaimed any consuming interest in theory, wishing "chiefly to bring out the

facts of this interesting and much neglected matter; and to indicate the additional delectation which attends the study of
them."[32] He proposed to proceed "by the application of the foot-
system—that is to say, by studying the combinations of the two
great sound-qualities which, for my part, I call, as my fathers
called them from the beginning, 'long' and 'short,' but which
you may call anything you like, so long as you observe the difference and respect the grouping. . . ."[33]

Although the actual foot-scansion in the *Prosody* stimulated
considerable controversy and much downright disagreement as
to the nature of English verse, it nevertheless had a traditional
basis that made it generally acceptable to the majority of readers,
even without Saintsbury's technical defenses of it both in the
history and in the prosodic *Manual*. The application of foot-
scansion to English prose, however, was far more of a novelty;
and although its logic and reasonableness, its consonance with
the facts, were brilliantly demonstrated, there were few among
those interested who could accept Saintsbury's method of ana-
lyzing how the effects of characteristic prose specimens were
achieved. There was some quarrel with, and much gratitude for,
the many actual examples contained in the book and for the
sensitive characterizations of styles.

"The first history of the theme," Elton wrote of the *Prose
Rhythm*, "it furnishes a multitude of scanned and commented
examples, and of nice analyses and judgments." But, he added,
"it is a history and a body of criticism rather than a theory. . . ."[34]
In the same essay Elton pointed out that "Professor Saintsbury,
like many others, uses quantity-marks in scanning English,
though he carefully avoids dogmatizing on the physics or physiology of the question."[35] And again: "Can we thus throw light
on the special rhythm, the distinctive beauty or pleasure, furnished by different writers or by different sorts of prose? Professor Saintsbury's *History* is one long effort to discriminate such
effects and to find words for them. He has much that is new to
teach, and he will sharpen many impressions that were dim before, if indeed they were present to us at all."[36]

The "physics or physiology of the question" has occupied many
critics and investigators before and since; but deeper, more per-
spicacious insights into English prose have been lacking. "The

scientific study of English prose rhythm, despite the very complete and provocative history devoted to it by Professor Saintsbury," wrote Herbert Read, "is still very much in its infancy."[37] "What is a complete rhythm," he asks, "what constitutes its essence, why once begun does it continue for a definite course and come to an appointed end? This is the question which Professor Saintsbury did not ask himself, and it is, indeed, perhaps the most difficult question in the whole complex of English prose style."[38]

These are the kinds of questions Saintsbury avoided as he avoided fools, for they are not even "scientific." He had no quarrel with, though he had little admiration for, the "scientific" investigation itself of such matters, so long as no claims were made to explain the inexplicable, or to recommend measurements and formulas as substitutes for ears and eyes. With respect to "sound-photography" and other mechanical devices and gadgets for investigating prose and poetry, the procedure, he says,

may tell us something about the physical-psychological characteristics of the individual experimenting, or being experimented upon. It may provide fresh material for that individual's dossier, to be registered and stored by a new Government Department. But on no passage of Chaucer or of Swinburne, of Malory or of Ruskin, can it shed the very dimmest light as to its structure, arrangement, or rhythmical quality. The results of the machinery remain as remote from literature as the machinery itself; while, even as regards these results, the tyranny of individuality retains its scornful predominance. Each intelligent observer, patient, subject, or whatever he is to be termed, can whisper to himself, "At the next examination, if I choose, I can upset my record utterly."[39]

What the senses, controlled and cultivated by mind and experience, tell us may be, after all, false; but it *can* be true. When science validly contradicts experience, the senses will, if we are not idiotic, adjust accordingly, but science cannot tell us *what* to experience.

Further, the flaw in all mechanical attempts to analyze the prose rhythms of English writers by vocalizing their words lies in the fact that writing and speech are not identical; and, whereas a good piece of written prose is unlikely to make any voice worse than it is, the human voice can rarely do even approximate justice to such prose as delights the inner ear directly from the printed page. Neither rhythm nor the silent sounds of words can be transferred into the audible without the destruction of the subtleties proper to them, although by means of trained voices *other* subtleties proper to speech may take their places.

The main objections to *Prose Rhythm* stemmed not only from the absence in the book of any recognition of the value of other possible approaches to the subject, but also from Saintsbury's considered rejection of existing differences of approach. He proclaimed merely that "as the essence of verse-metre is its identity (at least in equivalence) and recurrence, so the essence of prose-rhythm lies in variety and divergence."[40] And again: "As in reference to *Prosody,* so in reference to *Prose Rhythm,* I disclaim, detest, abominate, and in every other English and classical form renounce, the attempt to show how a prose-harmonist should develop his harmony. But I hope that I may perhaps have shown, and may now show farther, how the harmonists of the past have developed theirs."[41] That aim was his full purpose. He staunchly refused to recognize a "scientific" examination of *literature as literature,* or any other examination that by-passed or ignored the principal reason for its existence: its appeal to the mind and the emotions of a reader, whatever his interests, stands on the basis of a shared humanity. Saintsbury by no means dismissed the use of literature as material for the exploration of non-literary elements, sociological, historical, psychological, or philological; he drew the line only when the discoveries of such explorations were used to *explain,* or even to *describe,* the literature. Since Saintsbury's day this procedure has become, as he foresaw, more and more common, more and more *de rigueur;* and the public that reads the Classics has dwindled until it consists mainly of students upon whom they are imposed and of the tyrants themselves, the teachers, the scholars, the experimenters, and the theses-writers. The question as to who benefits from this approach remains unanswered, unless we accept the fact that the beneficiary is that amorphous and less and less culturally significant *recitativo secco* called "the world of learning."

Some critics have preferred exclamation over the indisputable quantity of Saintsbury's reading to a recognition of his obvious, unique mastery of his subjects. That mastery is nowhere more evident than in the histories we have been considering and in the ones to come.

IV A Place of Rest and Refreshment

The Peace of the Augustans, A Survey of Eighteenth Century Literature as a Place of Rest and Refreshment[42] is usually included with the previously discussed histories as the penultimate of Saintsbury's major works. Major it is, but it is not a history in the sense that the other books are, nor does Saintsbury call it one. It is what the title and subtitle imply: an extended and completely idiosyncratic survey of eighteenth-century English writers in their time and place, and in their roles as contributors to the rest and refreshment of a thoroughly independent scholar now in his seventies. Saintsbury himself modestly says in the preface that "he has given the usual *History of Eighteenth Century Literature* with a difference."[43] And this *difference* is unique. It is an unusual book, unlike any other of his own or other men's. It bulges with the kind of enthusiasm that is rare even in youth, with unexpected judgments favorable and unfavorable, and with infinite sidelights, digressions, and reflections on "matter and thought and temperament." A beautiful book, it is by far one of the best works extant about a century that has interested modern writers as much as any. Originally published by George Bell & Sons in 1916, in 1946 it was thought worthy of inclusion in the Oxford World's Classics where it carries a curiously qualified "Introduction" by H. J. C. Grierson, who took over from Saintsbury at Edinburgh in October, 1915, the date affixed to Saintsbury's original preface.

Grierson is far from unappreciative of his predecessor—"for no critic was ever more human, less pedantic,"[44] he says; and "the book has all the characteristics of Saintsbury's literary criticism —the extraordinary gusto with which he wrote of whatever gave him pleasure, unabated by years and indeed brought into clearer relief from the fact that he is dealing with a period some aspects of which he thoroughly enjoyed while of one of its special glories in its own eyes he was, with the best will in the world, *not* a whole-hearted admirer."[45] Yet Grierson spends most of the space at his disposal in drawing the prospective reader's attention to

Saintsbury's limitations, to "two characteristics which explain its
[Saintsbury's criticism] attractiveness to many readers and to
some indicate certain limitations."[46] It is difficult to see that the
first of these indicates "certain limitations": "literature was for
him one, if poetry perhaps the chief, of the good things this
world has to give us. He judged it simply and frankly by the
pleasure which it gave him, as he judged of wine and food."[47]
That estimate sounds a bit as if Grierson were addressing a
seminary.

The second characteristic, "Saintsbury's doctrine of the form,
and the form only," although Grierson holds it to be "in the
main incontestable,"[48] is, at length, oddly misrepresented in this
Introduction. In the first place, Saintsbury neither believed in
nor exemplified in actual practice any doctrine of "the form,
and the form only." What Saintsbury reiterates throughout his
critical work is merely that form is *primary;* that it clothes substance and makes it art; that the appreciation or disapproval of
substance is irrelevant to the consideration of the quality of
literature *as* literature, of the quality of poetry *as* poetry; and
that it is the *form* the substance takes, or is given, that reveals
the quality, if any, of the work under consideration. "Art for
art's sake," as a notion, may have sheltered disorganized minds
and small abilities at one time or another. That is no reflection
on the viewpoint itself, which is the only possible one even for
propaganda, even for didacticism and polemic, if it is to be art.
Such a viewpoint is *necessary,* moreover, to the critical mind.
The writer may completely reject it, or he may be quite uncon-
cerned with or unconscious of it in his preoccupation with entirely other purposes and objects. To judge what he accomplishes
as a writer, however, it does not do merely to be in or out of
sympathy with his purpose or object. The form of his accomplishment is primary to the judgment, and it must be examined and
assessed. In the process, substance or subject matter is *not* excluded, as any page of Saintsbury's will demonstrate; it is simply
kept separate to whatever extent is possible. In the greatest art,
the union of form and substance is perfect and absolute. *The
Peace of the Augustans* is a superb illustration of this critical
process; and there again Saintsbury in his Preface, explains what
should be self-evident—were critics not so often more interested

in theory than in fact. Eight years later he once more touches upon the subject briefly in an essay on "Early Twentieth Century Literature": "When the force is only in the matter it may not exactly lose all its power, but certainly finds that power what the financial people call 'a wasting asset'."[49]

That the idea of "art for art's sake" can still produce exercises in muddled pedantry and passionate protest is evidence that the genuine artist is still an unwelcome phenomenon. Perhaps the confusion will never be cleared, though it is hard to see that there is a real problem here. We know, surely, that the artist is in one or another position with regard to his materials; they compel him, or he compels them. In the first case, he cannot be said to have any purpose beyond obedience to the mute demands of the substance with which he works: ideas, words, sound, movement. Whatever the realized quality and the fate of his work, this situation is plainly "art for art's sake." In the second case, we have to ask the artist *why* he is imposing himself on the materials, and to this question there can be many answers. He may like the struggle: this may be called pedantry. He may be bent on making himself feel important, victorious: this is vanity, and dangerous. Or he may wish to impress his friends or the public: this, at one end of the scale, is compromise; at the other, degradation.

Or to state the case another way: to the best of our insights and abilities, we show our respect for all that is external to us by careful and accurate recognition of it in its character and particularities, by an honorable confrontation of the world that has made and is making us. And we then respond boldly, freely, and securely to its demands. This is the artist's view, whether conscious or instinctive; and his art is consequently for "art's sake." For the rest of us, his art is merely there, a voluntary offering. The contrary view supports the inordinate cherishing of ourselves to the exclusion of all that might disturb us; so that what we do, as artists, is for our own comfort, prestige, and success. This is art for our own sakes, however it may be disguised as for the sake of others.

The Peace of the Augustans remains a constant delight to anyone interested in the great figures of eighteenth-century literature; and, along with the great, the reader's appetite is whetted for a host of minors of whom he may have known only what held him off from them. "The mood is given," wrote A. Blyth Webster, by, among other things, "the fact that for combination of humour, wisdom, melancholy, and manliness his absolute admiration and whole-hearted assent go to Swift, to Fielding, to Johnson, and to them alone. . . ."[50]

J. B. Priestley found *The Peace of the Augustans* "bristling" with "crotchets." Now "crotchets" are defined as *whimsical fancies*, of which some felt that Saintsbury was unusually free. Yet Priestley experienced much of the quality of the book, for he said:

But even in this volume, where he makes very unfair though entertaining comparisons between an eighteenth century that he clearly understands and loves and a twentieth century that he plainly does not care to understand and love—even here he performs his task supremely well; it is his business to comment upon the literature of the older century, and this he does magnificently. Crotchets or no crotchets, not once does he play the traitor to his love of letters; not once does he deny the Muse and conceal his delight or find none, because of extra-literary considerations. On the other hand, there are not a few writers whose characters are the very ones with which he is least likely to have any sympathy, whose views and aims must be abhorrent to him, to whom he has been one of the first to do full justice.[51]

For perhaps obscure reasons, enthusiasm for Saintsbury's work embarrasses the enthusiast as often as not; and one extreme statement is frequently canceled out by something very like its opposite. *The Peace of the Augustans*, wrote Robert Lynd, "is an almost irresistible incitement to go and forget the present world among the poets and novelists and biographers and letter-writers of the eighteenth century."[52] Many readers have found this assessment to be strictly true. But to Lynd, Saintsbury's "estimates of authors are the impressions of a man talking in a hurry, and his method is the method of exaggeration rather than of precise statement. How deficient he is in the sense of proportion may be judged from the fact that he devotes slightly more space to Collins than to Pope, unless the pages in which he assails 'Grub Street' as a malicious invention of Pope's are to be counted to the credit of the latter."[53] Now specific and reasoned praise of a minor author is not to be counted "exaggeration" because one does not agree with it; nor is the allocation of space in a book such as *The Peace of the Augustans* to be held as showing a deficiency in "the sense of proportion." Who establishes those laws of proportion which *require* that Pope be considered at greater length than Collins?

And again, Lynd said—and this statement, oddly gratuitous, sounds more as if it were addressed to schoolboys than to the "general reader": "At the same time, it is only fair to warn the general reader not to follow Mr. Saintsbury's recommendations and opinions too blindly."[54] And finally, for Lynd *is* an admirer of Saintsbury, "however one may quarrel with it, *The Peace of the Augustans* is a book to read with delight—an eccentric book, an extravagant book, a grumpy book, but a book of rare and amazing enthusiasm for good literature."[55] Oliver Elton described it differently: Saintsbury "flings away his gown, and writes exactly as he likes, and exactly as he talked and corresponded. He is heedless of the canons, and of the censors who for years had thrown up their hands at his 'style.' The general public now began to be aware of a veteran who was full, to use a word of his own, of 'sempervirescence'."[56]

This "richly-talked"[57] book reveals its qualities no matter where it is sampled. Of a major figure, Saintsbury writes:

Common sense salted and spirited with humour; inflexible principle combined with utmost charity; wide knowledge without pedantry (the notion of Johnson as a typical pedant probably still survives, but only in the poorest wits, unenriched with even the slightest knowledge); curiosity again tempered by a wholesome scepticism which applied to all things provable, while it respected things where proof is not in place; pride, in that sense where pride is no deadly sin—indeed no sin at all—because it has been tried seven and seventy times in the fire of suffering, and purged of all the dross of vanity; a courage mental, moral, and physical, utterly fearless of every person and everything but God and God's doomsman Death; other good things that could be catalogued almost to weariness—all are to be found in Johnson, and most of them are, as has been said, specific for the opposite qualities so common in our day.[58]

In a footnote to the phrase "the ethical-aesthetic," Saintsbury states: "As the present writer has always been a steady protester against those who would confuse Art and Morality this phrase may seem inconsistent, but it is not. Art has its own morality— a pretty severe and complicated one. It is sometimes called 'Taste'."[59]

And of one of Cowper's preferences, Saintsbury says:

His subjects were occasionally inadequate; he was right to be fond of fish, but a poet who can celebrate halibut must lack some of that discrimination which should be characteristic of the poetical character. In the eighteenth century dwellers inland had to take what they could get in the way of what the French delightfully call *marée*—a term which surrounds the actual fish with the sound and the sight and the smell of the sea. But when there are not only salmon and trout, turbot and brill, John Dory and mullet, but whiting and whitebait and sole and herring and flounders and sprats—nay even plaice and bass and skate and gurnet and other worthy if second-rate fish—to eat and to celebrate in verse a thing which is at best a cooked cotton counterpane, is shocking.[60]

Or of Richardson, Saintsbury succinctly comments: "Richardson's admirers have described him as pitiless to his personages; some of his critics admit that he is so to his readers."[61]

In an assessment of the Addisonian essay, Saintsbury states:

The mightier and more soul-stirring raptures—the voices of the mountain and the sea—are not indeed with us; they are in fact *ex hypothesi* excluded, and if you want them you must go elsewhere. But you are in a sort of Happy Valley with a pleasant town-capital in its center, to the streets of which you are by no means confined. You may make excursions to woods and fields with a village not too far off, where a decent meal can be obtained. If town and country do not fully suffice, there is literature for you—not quite all literature, but a fair proportion both of ancient and modern, some art (though you do not take this very seriously), a little science, and at intervals passages of perfectly sincere if not very enthusiastic or exalted piety. A "middle" style of everything perhaps; but a happy mean enough—amusing almost always, if only from its contrasts with or its curious anticipations of the present, full of an agreeable decency "in the best sense of the term" (as a late Master of Balliol used to say when he wished to be apparently complimentary but really meaningless), and therefore not ill to dwell with, if not quite to dwell with for ever.[62]

These examples provide some idea of the manner and matter of this extraordinary book. If Saintsbury was not "a whole-hearted admirer" of the eighteenth century, the reader is scarcely aware of it. There were in its writers an astonishing variety of achievements to excite his enthusiasm—and innumerable corners from which his exploring mind brought forth delightful, amusing, and curious material. And, when it was necessary to condemn, he did it with a vigor, grace, and justness that made it as stirring in its way as his praise. On the great figures—Johnson, Fielding, Swift, and Pope—Saintsbury exhibited at its best that at once delicate and robust skill perfected by a lifetime of practice. He had a ranging splendor of recognition and appreciation that speaks of these men as they are and extenuates nothing. The most disagreeable of critics would find it hard to justify any serious disagreement, and only a sluggish mind could fail to enjoy the book and benefit by the enjoyment.

V *The Novel*

That once wicked phenomenon with a thousand-year history, the French novel, provided Saintsbury with the substance of the last of his big works, *A History of the French Novel* (*to the Close of the 19th Century*). It came out in two volumes in 1917-19, and it was his "farewell to literary history, and a superbly generous installment, and sample of his method."[63] Saintsbury was in his seventies, and his subject was "one with which I can at least plead almost lifelong familiarity." He opens his preface as follows:

In beginning what, if it ever gets finished, must in all probability be the last of some already perhaps too numerous studies of literary history, I should like to point out that the plan of it is somewhat different from that of most, if not all, of its predecessors. I have usually gone on the principle (which I still think a sound one) that, in studying the literature of a country, or in dealing with such general characteristics of parts of literature as prosody, or such coefficients of all literature as criticism, minorities are, sometimes at least, of as much importance as majorities, and that to omit them altogether is to risk, or rather to assure, an imperfect—and dangerously imperfect—product.

In the present instance, however, I am attempting something that I have never, at such length, attempted before—the history of a Kind, and a Kind which has distinguished itself, as few others have done, by communicating to readers the *pleasure* of literature. I might almost say that it is the history of that pleasure, quite as much as the history of the kind itself, that I wish to trace. In doing so it is obviously super-fluous to include inferiorities and failures, unless they have some very special lesson or interest, or have been (as in the case of the minorities on the bridge of the sixteenth and seventeenth centuries) for the most part, and unduly, neglected, though they are important as experiments and links. We really do want here—what the reprehensible hedonism of Mr. Matthew Arnold, and his submission to what some one has called "the eternal enemy, Caprice," wanted in all cases—"only the chief and principal things." I wish to give a full history of how what is commonly called the French Novel came into being and kept itself in being; but I do not wish to give an exhaustive, though I hope to give a pretty full, account of its practitioners.[64]

Saintsbury took "novel" to include "not only the prose books, old and new, which are more generally called 'romance,' but [also] the verse romances of the earliest period." He began with the *Chanson de Geste* and closed, more than a thousand generous pages later, with Catulle Mendès. And throughout most of the first volume he provided his own translation of illustrative passages from the verse and prose romances and novels under consideration.

The result is, to some tastes, the most delightful of his books. The critical and comparing eye is as watchful as ever, and "that enthusiasm, with its train of half-humorous and wholly admirable hyperboles,"[65] is more richly present than ever before. Elton called the *History* a "commentary upon the French genius that is not excelled in its union of range with flexible sympathy."[66] One might like to know in what book or books it is even remotely equaled.

Few of us could possibly read the library of French literature with such relish as Saintsbury read it, yet the pleasure in what of it is read is immeasurably increased and heightened, both in retrospect and in anticipation, by his lavish historical and comparative account of the total. The *French Novel* is the sole comprehensive resource for English readers interested in the subject. A critical reader of "fiction" in a foreign language, from the *fabliau* to Zola, with such an appetite as Saintsbury's is un-likely to have a successor; and he had no predecessor. Such a reader would be even more unlikely to have Saintsbury's astonishing grasp of comparison and contrast in half a dozen literatures and languages. This detailed acquaintance with all varieties of French writing, together with comparable familiarity with Classical and other modern literatures, gives the *History of the French Novel* its interpretive depth along with its obvious surface vivacity and extraordinary range of reference and allusion. I know of few books more amusing to read, and the reader who wants a controlled and intelligible perspective on the kinds of "fictions" produced by the imagination of man has no other equally instructive and delightful source to go to.

The work met with the usual criticism from both specialists and cranks and, of course, there were those occasional errors of fact, omissions, and confusions which, in such herculean ingatherings, Saintsbury himself—and every reasonable person—expected. The ability to correct mere error of fact is in everyone's hands. Saintsbury wrote no books of reference, although most of his larger works were constantly used as such. But what is more to the point, he was rarely, if ever, wrong in his descriptions and assessments; and he himself freely admitted reasonable differences of opinion in areas of taste and preference. With his own eye on the subject, he was content to invite the reader's eye to it.

In the *French Novel* Saintsbury gave more than six detailed pages to the brothers Goncourt, and he selected *Germinie Lacerteux* for a brief summary of the story. His conclusions, based on the novels, the brothers' theories of Naturalism, and their *Journal* were negative. He found *Germinie* "untouched and unconfirmed by the very slightest art; as destitute of any aesthetic attraction, or any evidence of artistic power, as the log-books of a common lodging-house and a hospital ward could be."[67] He cited a few details from the *Journal* and described it as "being saturated, larded, or whatever word of the kind be preferred, with observations on the taste, intellect, and general greatness of the MM. de Goncourt, and on the lamentable inferiority of other people, etc., etc. If it could be purged of its bad blood, the book would really deserve to rank, for substance, with Pepys's diary or with Walpole's letters."[68]

This estimate is cited at some length because it is dismissed by a partisan writer in these words: "Even in Professor Saintsbury's enormous and catholic survey of the French novel," Ernest Boyd wrote of the Goncourts, "they receive a few intolerant paragraphs, in which indignation takes the place of criticism and historical perspective."[69] This statement is not so; the clash is one of taste, not of judgment. Saintsbury saw more or less just what Boyd saw in the Goncourts. The difference is that, with a genuine "historical perspective," Saintsbury did not regard their work as literature. Boyd's perspective was that of 1925—and since then far grubbier works than those of the Goncourts have been celebrated.

There were numerous other criticisms of a similar kind: writers such as Hugo who were held in disesteem in some quarters were therefore overrated by Saintsbury; and there were writers who had come into temporary fashion to whom Saintsbury inexcusably did not do justice. Despite such expected carping, the *French Novel* was more widely read than the earlier histories; the subject was of more general interest, and there was no competitive treatment in either French or English.

Saintsbury also wrote a book on *The English Novel*, an historical study of its development from its "foundation in romance" to William Morris. It preceded the volumes on the *French Novel* and appeared in 1913 in a series, "The Channels of English Literature," in which that literature is treated by categories: epic and heroic poetry, lyric poetry, essays and essayists, historians and schools of history, etc., each by a different authority.

Saintsbury's volume, oddly enough, was the first in English to deal with such a subject and, as good a book as it is, one may regret that he did not have the freedom to deal, as he wished, with the English novel at length and in the manner in which he was subsequently to deal with the French. As it is, in addition to fulfilling its purpose admirably, the book is full of the expected good things. This one, for example: "just as the excessive desire to be *like* all the best models is the note of Classical decadence, so the excessive desire to be *unlike* everything else is the note of Romantic degeneration."[70] Or, from among many others, is this statement about Jane Austen: "The value of her, artistically, is of course in the perfection of what she did; but the value of her historically is in the way in which she showed that, given the treatment, any material could be perfected."[71]

CHAPTER 3

Editor anb Scholar

A GREAT deal of nonsense has been written about Saintsbury's scholarship. He was not, and at no time pretended to be, a scholar in the current twentieth-century, academic sense of the term. He was fifty-five years old when our century began and had already fully brought to maturation the kind of scholarship honored in the nineteenth century: the comprehensive training in and knowledge of Classical and modern languages and literatures. The specialization that has been substituted for this training in our own day was looked at askance by Saintsbury who was sceptical both of its purposes and its results. He also had little use for literary pedigrees. In his introduction to *Tristan in Brittany* he wrote: "I have said, perhaps too often, that I do not enter into questions of literary origin and connection. I confess that the sight of those too familiar pedigrees, dangling down the page like strings of sausages but not nearly so nourishing or succulent as *good* sausages, has never delighted me in any way; while, speaking from my purely critical experience, which is not very small, I seldom find them justified or useful."[1] He fully respected, however, that technical scholarship which was part, although not a necessary one, of the older idea of learning, and he repeatedly acknowledged that it had never been his strong point.[2] In his old age, for various reasons—a uniquely crowded memory and lifelong poor eyesight among them—it all but deserted him. He had no interest at all in what he called "antiquarian punctilio," and he was well aware that "those who place philology, archaeology, and other things ancillary to literature, above literature itself,"[3] would quarrel with him.

I Editions

His edition of Walter Scott's edition of Dryden's works, from which the above quotation is taken, was proposed to him by the Edinburgh publisher, William Paterson. The eighteen volumes appeared between 1882 and 1893, but most of the actual work was completed with the publication of the earlier volumes. Mark Van Doren called it "unfortunately as well as fortunately a monument," and he unaccountably added that "it never has lent itself to familiar handling."[4] The volumes are not pocket books, but they are not so bulky as Montague Summers' later edition of the plays. Moreover, they are excellent examples of handsome printing in large type. The edition is by far the most pleasant one in which to read through Dryden's works.

As texts, however, these volumes have a poor reputation, mainly because Saintsbury had no intention of following the rules of editing that became obligatory only fifty years later. He committed such blunders as the modernization of orthography and punctuation, and he otherwise tampered with the text in order to make it easier to read. He tried to keep as close to Scott's edition as seemed reasonable to him, and he made much use of Christie's improvements. His purpose and procedure were clearly set forth in his various prefaces to parts of the work.

Saintsbury produced an edition for the general reader, not for future scholars. Textual scholarship, however, did not ignore it. When John Sargeaunt came to prepare an edition of the poems for Oxford, he acknowledged the unusual difficulty of establishing an authoritative text. At the same time, he rammed the bulk of his own scholarship into the entire line of Dryden editors, Broughton, Derrick, Scott, the Wartons, Mitford, Hooper, Bell, Christie, and Saintsbury. To the last of these offenders Sargeaunt devoted the larger part of his introduction. He began by saying: "However well Dr. Saintsbury may have deserved of Dryden in other respects, it must be regretfully declared that his work on the text was worse than useless,"[5] and he provided supporting evidence. But, when Summers' edition of the plays appeared in 1931, it was Sargeaunt's turn to be criticized. His edition of the poems, says Summers, "must be used with much caution. The work is incomplete; there are gravest inaccuracies, and what is worse, unpardonable abridgements and deliberate excisions."[6]

For Saintsbury, however, Summers—the most eccentric, meticulous, and ill-natured of editors—called out his heavy artillery:

I have no hesitation in saying that this reprint of 1882-1893 is the worst edition of any considerable English author I know. There are blunders which a scholar may make: ill-health, weariness, failing eyesight, the inability to read proofs with precision, will all play sad tricks with one's work. But there are blunders no scholar can make, and in these latter Mr. Saintsbury's recension is extremely prolific. We have notes which are the merest guess-work, the idlest hazard; flat assertions demonstrably untrue; we have readings which occur in no edition of Dryden that can be traced and glosses to bolster up the error; worst of all we have a fudge title-page, that of *The State of Innocence* which, relying on a mistake of Malone, is presented as 1674. The first quarto was 1677.[7]

The mistake was made not only by Malone, but by Scott, David Masson, A. W. Ward, and W. C. Ward. But what is delightful here, and serves to show, for better or worse, Saintsbury's attitude toward what he considered of small consequence, is Summers' footnote: "When Mr. Saintsbury was asked where a copy of this 1674 quarto could be seen, he merrily turned off the inquiry by saying that this edition 'is probably a Boojum!' "[8] It is almost needless to say that, when Summers' turn came, he was faulted on the same grounds of textual scholarship which he had used to denigrate almost everyone who had even a remote connection with the text of Dryden. In addition, his manners were found reprehensible. And in the end, Augustus Muir was to call Saintsbury "the greatest exponent of Dryden in the whole history of criticism."[9]

Saintsbury edited numerous texts both before and after the Scott *Dryden*: an anthology of *French Lyrics* (1882); a series of seven French prose and dramatic classics for college students (1882-88); a volume of *Specimens of French Literature* (1883) as a companion to his *History; Specimens of English Prose Style* (1885); Swift's *Polite Conversation* (1892); *Loci Critici* to supplement his *History of Criticism* (1903); the Mermaid Series, *Shadwell* (1903) and *Dryden* (1904); three volumes of *Minor Poets of the Caroline Period* (1905-21); *A Letter Book* (1922); and editions of Fielding (1893), Herrick (1893), Sterne (1894), Balzac (1895-98), Smollett (1895-1900), and Thackeray (1908).

The only one of these editions that requires extended notice is the compendious three-volume *Caroline Poets* since, for the text of one of the poets, Sidney Godolphin, Saintsbury again brought forth scholarly criticism. He undertook this work for a number of reasons: his devotion to poetry, major and minor; his conviction that "the neglect of minorities is a serious . . . mistake";[10] his wish to make some eighteen poets of a past period again available to readers; and finally his desire to express his gratitude to Oxford University. The minor Caroline poets, Chamberlayne, Benlowes, Marmion, Ayres, King, Stanley, and the others, are undoubtedly not for everyone; they are, in fact, for those to whom the exploration of the world of poetry extends to its very boundaries. To such readers, these poets are of special interest not only for their frequent felicities of expression but also for their linguistic and historical characteristics, particularly, their relation to greater poets before and since. Nor is their subject-matter without interest.

As we have noted, Saintsbury had indicated his principles of editing in the Scott *Dryden*; and they were not such as would now be approved. But were he alive today, it is unlikely that he would have much altered or modified them. He wrote in his preface to the two-volume *Herrick*:

There is, I believe, an idea prevalent, rather with a certain class of critics than with the public, that an elaborate commentary, stuffed with parallel passages and other ostentations of erudition, is a guarantee of scholarship on the part of the editor. From some experience I am inclined to feel considerable doubts on this point, but even if I felt none I should not be disposed to emulate the athletes of copious annotation. For I desire in all things to treat others as I would be treated myself, and nothing is to me such an intolerable nuisance as an edition of a classic where the eye and the mind are constantly called off the text in order to do reason to the comment.[11]

In the *Caroline Poets,* in the introduction to Edward Benlowes, he said:

I am, of course, well aware that there is, as there has long been, a habit of demanding adherence to original spelling, and of regarding those editions which comply with this demand as "scholarly," and those which do not as "slovenly." I disagree with the opinion and decline to comply with the demand. As a matter of fact, the retention of the old spelling gives the editor very little trouble, and the alteration of it a very great deal. But this is nothing. In the first place there is no real reason, in the case of any writer at any rate later than the beginning of the seventeenth century, for throwing in the way of the modern reader an unnecessary obstacle to enjoyment. In the second place, and in the case of such authors as those with whom we are now dealing, the advantage of the original spelling, even to the severest reader for knowledge and not enjoyment, is almost infinitesimally small.[12]

Except when Saintsbury was preparing school texts, he edited works of literature largely for the enjoyment of the interested reader and not for the compliments of the exact scholar or the textual critic. Many aspects of scholarship were, if not beyond his competence, certainly beyond his patience and his purpose; and he was quite willing to leave such matters to those who found them congenial. With the *Caroline Poets,* his problem was to get as many as possible of the poets into print with as little fuss as possible, with a minimum of editorial matter, and with only such annotation as might either amuse the reader or assist the reading. In a note to the General Introduction to Volume I, he said:

The principles of editing which have been adopted can be very shortly set forth. In all cases, whether the texts have been set up from reprints, as in a few cases, or from the originals, as in most, they have been carefully collated with these originals themselves and all important variations noted, and where necessary explained. The spelling has been subjected to the very small amount of modernization necessary to make it uniform with the only uniformity which is at all possible. At this time no texts were printed with very antique spelling, and some present for whole pages nothing that is not modern, except an occasional capital Initial. A very few readers might prefer the reproduction of anomalous and contradictory archaisms; but these would certainly repel a much larger number, and interfere with the acquaintance which it is desired to bring about. With regard to punctuation, the fantastic and irregular clause—and sentence—architecture of the time hardly admits of a strict application of any system. This is partly remedied, or at least recognized, in the originals by an extremely liberal use of the semicolon, which has been generally retained, except where means of improvement are obvious. Glossarial notes have been added where they seemed necessary or very desirable, but with a sparing hand; and notes, explanatory of matter, with a hand more sparing still. The object constantly kept in view by the editor has been the provision, not of biographical, bibliographical, or commentatorial minutiae, but of a sufficient and trustworthy text for the student and the lover of literature.[13]

In order to include Sidney Godolphin in the second volume, however, Saintsbury had to work for the most part from manuscripts, there being no previous edition; and his weak eyes betrayed him. In the third volume he made his apology as follows:

The eye-weakness just mentioned having always prevented me from making any regular study of palaeography, I had originally proposed only to include work already printed. I was tempted to break my rule in the case of Godolphin: and made rather a mess of it. An errata list in the present volume . . . will, I believe, repair the blunder. The single censurer of this (I further believe) single serious lapse of mine was, I remember, troubled about it as a discredit to the University of Oxford. I sincerely trust that he was mistaken. None of us can possibly do credit to our University; we can only derive it from her. To throw any discredit on her is equally impossible: though of course any member may achieve such discredit for himself. Let me hope that the balance against me for indiscreet dealing with perhaps one per cent. of my fifteen hundred or two thousand pages is not too heavy.[14]

For this third volume, which appeared in 1921 when Saintsbury was seventy-six, he required the editorial help provided by Percy Simpson and Thorn-Drury, whom he acknowledged as "part-editors" of the text. When the text of Godolphin was re-edited by William Dighton in 1931, John Drinkwater, who prefaced the book, had this to say of Saintsbury's "indiscreet dealing": "Modern textual scholarship has had some hard things to say of this work, but the fact remains that it is an invaluable reassembling of forgotten things, that it was possible only to Professor Saintsbury's poetic erudition, and that it is distinguished everywhere by his unfailing poetic judgment. Of all modern critics of poetry, there is none, I think, who over so large a field is so consistently right as he."[15]

That statement, I submit, can stand. I have given the extended extracts above from Saintsbury's remarks on his editing because they show forthrightly the manner of man he was, and not only as critic, editor, historian, and writer; and they show it far better and more clearly than any paraphrase or condensation of their substance could. They also illustrate his consistently practical and common-sense attitude toward problems whose solutions others have often made into ends in themselves.

As to the Caroline poets themselves, opinion has been sharply enough divided. To René Wellek the three volumes of the *Minor Poets of the Caroline Period* are filled with a "mass of quibbling conceited verse."[16] To John Drinkwater, "to care for poetry is, I think, to find scarcely one page too many in the nearly two thousand of that masterly piece of devoted scholarship and taste."[17] Quibbles and conceits are not necessarily the dreadful things they are made out to be by the unimaginative. Remove them from verse—remove them in all their incredibly varied forms from Shakespeare—and there is not a great deal left.

Two other editing projects require mention. Saintsbury's *Thackeray* (1908) is one of the two most agreeable editions of that novelist, the other being Lady Ritchie's "Biographical" edition published earlier; and Saintsbury's edition has the advantage of being in pocket-size volumes, seventeen of them. Fortunately, the various prefaces were extracted and separately printed in a single volume—a suggestion made originally in 1910 by Austin Dobson—as *A Consideration of Thackeray* (1931). Saintsbury's prefaces to the forty volumes of the *Balzac* (1895-98) equally deserve, but so far have been denied, separate republication. Arnold Bennett, so scornful of Saintsbury's style and knowledge —"a regular Albert Memorial of learning,"[18] considered them "startlingly just";[19] and Frank Swinnerton thought them "the best things of their kind."[20]

II Last Works

Late in life Saintsbury wrote his last four books which, oddly enough considering their nature, extended his reputation far beyond the confines to which it had been held by his critical and historical writing. All four, noted in one literary history as "certain books of a mixed and indescribable kind,"[21] contained criticism and history, but with a difference. They were *Notes on a Cellar-Book* (1920), *A Scrap Book* (1922), *A Second Scrap Book* (1923), and *A Last Scrap Book* (1924).

Readers of Saintsbury's essays and histories were well aware of his extensive knowledge of and discriminating interest in food and wine; for, among other delightful aspects of his serious work treating of Classical, medieval, and modern literature, were the amusing amplifications and asides connected with his authors' references to such matters. Saintsbury had, in fact, early contributed to two volumes in a series of books for sportsmen: to one, a chapter on the cookery of the partridge; to the other, on the cookery of the grouse.[22] The *Notes on a Cellar-Book* itself gave readers the benefit of Saintsbury's extensive direct and historical knowledge of alcoholic drinks; and along with this information—since the United States had become "dry" and England itself had its share of impuritans anxious to prohibit what they could—he properly chastised, ridiculed, and dismissed all teetotalers, meddlers, and do-gooders. Further, the book was full of literature itself, as any writing by Saintsbury was bound to be. It became, for the work of a retired scholar, quite popular and went into several editions, including a posthumous American one (1933) with a preface by Owen Wister.[23]

For readers with a varied and discriminating appetite for wines and other alcoholic drinks, for "the world of judicious feasters,"[24] the book is a delight, if at times a teasing one; and it deserves its popularity. "Blue-noses," however, quite naturally objected; they were, in fact, nauseated at the prospect of an aged "gentleman and scholar" conducting such a blatantly enjoyable monologue. Philip Guedalla found Saintsbury's case "a distressing demonstration of the deadly efficacy of environment," and took the occasion to indulge in juvenile sarcasm and to demonstrate his own inability to read accurately when under the influence of, I presume, water.[25] Saintsbury took note of him in the third printing of the book merely as "one of the Pussyfoot *sbirri.*"[26]

The *Cellar-Book* is beyond criticism, but liking it is a matter of taste and interest. The scrap books, unfortunately, were partly of a nature to justify criticism, although they were most favorably received at the time of publication; and all those "hearties" who first discovered Saintsbury through the *Cellar-Book* bought and treasured them. In them, Saintsbury not only elaborated on his political beliefs as a stubborn Tory; but he chose, among other matters, labor unions and democracy as his objects for anything but dispassionate irony and invective. What he had to say on these subjects was inherent in his political faith. "He professes a creed of Toryism so extreme, so fantastic," wrote J. B. Priestley, "that it probably has no fellow in these islands."[27] Unfortunately, Saintsbury's faith had been moribund for nearly a hundred years and was, at the time he wrote, dead. When it revived, it revived elsewhere and was transformed. It had become fascism, a movement that would have thoroughly disgusted him.

Those who objected in print, then and later, to some of these "scraps," did so by imputing senility to Saintsbury. It is true that he was seventy-seven when the first installment appeared, but he would likely have expressed himself just as strongly, if not similarly, fifty years earlier. In fact, he did. It should not be forgotten that he was for many years a political journalist.

This book is not the place, however, to dwell upon Saintsbury's political views, if only because they in no way affected his judgments as an historian and critic. That in itself is an extraordinary critical accomplishment, and is acknowledged as such by even some of his most adverse critics. No one could have mistaken his indomitable views on non-literary matters when he chose to state them. They were strong enough to ravish the reason of any overserious radical who came upon them unprepared and to at least disconcert democratic liberals who may have had some interest in literature. "If there is a single seat of honour among those who discourse of Church and State," wrote his friend Elton, "that is *beyond* the extreme Right, there, surely, sits Saintsbury."[28]

Economists, political agitators, labor union leaders—these were only a few of the groups under attack in the scrap books; but the attacks on them are all but indefensible. On the other hand, Saintsbury, when he attacks educators, improvers, teetotalers, advocates of "progress," democratic snobbery, the "new" criticism, and a dozen other subjects, is not only defensible but exhilarating even to a democrat. The greater part of the scrap books consists, however, of reminiscence, marginalia on hundreds of matters, and little essays; and all these are delightful, amusing, and "a mirror of the real, the ultimate Saintsbury."[29] They and the *Cellar-Book* are the source of much of what we are permitted to know of his personal life. We learn, for example, from a note in the *Cellar-Book*, that he had more than one sister, though not how many more;[30] and, in the *Second Scrap Book*, that at least one of his sisters was already married when he was still at Oxford.[31] The scrap books are, further, full of that allusiveness which was and still is so petulantly objected to by those who have never been anything but the most special of specialists and by those who do not read.

The three scrap books are full of oddities and are themselves unclassifiable. They perhaps belong with such dissimilar but really kindred works as Southey's *The Doctor*, Burton's *Anatomy of Melancholy*, Norman Douglas' *Looking Back*, John Wilson's *Noctes Ambrosianae*, and Locker-Lampson's *Patchwork*.

Such books as these may no longer recommend themselves to readers. Their appeal, beyond their own day, cannot be expected to reach a large audience. They might regain some part of the attraction they have lost, however, were someone interested in and capable of hunting down and annotating the thousands of autobiographical, social, political, and literary allusions in them —and then of providing the volumes with adequate indices. But they will remain, as Saintsbury called them, "Scrap Books." In them the reader finds a series of exquisitely informal portraits of friends no longer living, which Saintsbury called "Little Necrologies"; extended "scraps" on the Oxford University of Saintsbury's youth; varied observations on the passing scenes of a long life, including the two decades of journalism; and individual pieces on everything from Virgil to the Phoenix Park Murder, from *Theagenes and Chariclea* to "Children," from the *Epistolae Obscurorum Virorum* to "Primerolatry." And everywhere there is evidence of Saintsbury's first love, poetry; and it is quoted and sometimes misquoted to the end.

CHAPTER 4

Style

"THE consideration of style," Saintsbury observed in his *History of Criticism*, "is at least half of criticism itself."[1] And again he wrote: "The style—the form—is that which the author adds to the matter; it is that inseparable but separably intelligible element which cannot be transferred, taken away or lost."[2] If Saintsbury is ever again read with the relish with which he was read during his life, it will be for his style. The materials of his histories and essays may be added to and corrected, or perhaps found to be of insufficient interest in themselves. In literature, as in the other arts, style is the sole preservative; it is really the only quality in writing that makes continued reading and re-reading across generations likely. Research and scholarship and reliable information have their proper and immediate virtues. They are not, however, the essential virtues of literature, which acquires its power to maintain a hold on the mind, imagination, and emotion of readers by its handling of language, its expressive character, and its intensity—and not by its subject matter.

I The Attacks and the Defense

Throughout his career, Saintsbury's style, or absence of style, was either attacked or regretted. In 1881 the poet Gerard Manley Hopkins wrote to another poet: "He writes a bad style, a vulgar style."[3] In 1886 Oscar Wilde said that Saintsbury was "a writer who seems quite ignorant of the commonest laws both of grammar and of literary expression. . . ."[4] In 1901 Churton Collins raged at "the offensive vulgarity of his diction and style—a very well of English defiled."[5] Fifty years later the secretary of the Saintsbury Club was quoted as saying of Saintsbury: "Unfortunately, he can't write English."[6]

In addition to the above observations, there was every variation of dismissal and of mere tolerance. Swinnerton said that "his literary manner is one of the worst known in the pre-Freudian era of literary criticism."[7] According to Ludwig Lewisohn, despite his praise for the "unaging vivacity, inexhaustible enthusiasm, delightful human warmth" of Saintsbury's pages, "it is perfectly true that Professor Saintsbury writes well in neither the older nor the newer sense."[8] And Arnold Bennett said that Saintsbury's style "is such that even in Carmelite Street the sub-editors would try to correct it."[9]

Wilde was more specific: Saintsbury "has as little hesitation in ending the clause of a sentence with a preposition, as he has in inserting a parenthesis between a preposition and its object, a mistake of which the most ordinary schoolboy would be ashamed."[10] Others have found Saintsbury's manner "rebarbative," "atrocious," "extremely tedious," "unfortunate," "slovenly and eccentric," and even "a non-style." And these are, if true, formidable objections. But, in view of the frequent enthusiastic praise of his critical faculty, I find it hard to understand the niggardly view of his style. Saintsbury himself made no claims whatever for his prose except such as were implicit in the facts that he continued to write, and that he wrote about style itself on more than one occasion. In this connection, Walter Pater, himself an acknowledged stylist but one now perhaps in eclipse, thought that Saintsbury's introductory essay to the *Specimens of English Prose Style* "might well stand, along with the best of these extracts from a hundred or more deceased masters of English, as itself a document or standard, in the matter of prose style."[11]

II Development and Characteristics

With practice and age, Saintsbury grew bolder; and it is doubtful that Pater, though he might still have approved, would have found the prose of the *History of the French Novel* and of *The Peace of the Augustans* suitable to serve as a "standard." Saintsbury's latest prose provided as unlikely a model as Johnson's, Gibbon's, or Carlyle's; and it was every bit as individual. Of this prose, following Saintsbury's retirement to Bath, when he was "no longer in any uniform, academic or scholastic, however admirably tailored, but in mufti," and could "walk at large," Oliver Elton wrote: "then, indeed, his style is *released*: he is in easy, odd, defiant, and bright apparel: —odd, not for oddness' sake, but for comfort's sake, and because the dress is all his own. This kind of writing is seen, above all, in his *Scrap-Books*: you may take it or leave it; if you like it, he is pleased; if not, he does not greatly care. It has certainly attracted not only many a scholar but many who read simply for pleasure and who enjoy the quips, and twirls, and sallies, and parentheses, and allusions."[12]

For in time Saintsbury's prose really gave the purists something to talk about. It gradually achieved its own complex brilliance and ease, leaving the measured, obedient, and dryly worded sentence and paragraph of contemporaries, including the younger critics, far behind. He essayed a prose character full of perils but one entirely and unmistakably his own. It grew, naturally and gradually, out of his activity and character, his knowledge and reading; his extraordinary memory; and, above all, out of the delight he took in what men and women of the past, real and imaginary, had had to say, and in how they had said it. As Lafcadio Hearn noted, "there is a great deal more in his sentences than you can imagine when you read them for the first time."[13] The result made Saintsbury one of the most widely allusive writers since Hazlitt; the most word-curious, parenthetical, and syntactically varied since the seventeenth century; surely one of the most conversational of expository writers, apart from novelists, in modern times. George Sampson described Saintsbury's style as "gnarled and knotty . . . with large assertions complicated by instant qualifications and sub-qualifications," and found it "really conversational in texture."[14]

Saintsbury delighted in circumlocutions. Anyone who cannot stomach periphrasis will dismiss Saintsbury's style for this reason alone. He could not avoid periphrasis because that was the way his mind functioned. He used it variously and amusingly. F. L. Lucas in his guide to "good English prose" picks a number of Saintsbury's paragraphs and sentences to pieces and among them is the following: "In Chalmers's large pages and compressed printing, they barely exceed the half-score, and do not reach the dozen." Lucas adds: "which means, I suppose, 'eleven?'" To which ironic supposition the only reply is, "Yes, indeed!"[15]

Saintsbury himself took little direct notice of objections to his style—unless it was "notice" that he continued on his own way. But in his observations on other writers, occasional statements suggest and even define his own bent and practice. Several of his earliest statements, from an essay on "Modern English Prose" in 1876, deserve notice. First is a definition of style: "Style is the choice and arrangement of language with only a subordinate regard to the meaning to be conveyed. Its parts are the choice of the actual words to be used, the further selection and juxtaposition of these words, the structure of the clauses into sentences, and the composition of the sentences into paragraphs. Beyond the paragraph style can hardly be said to go, but within that limit it is supreme."[16]

This definition is simple enough for a dictionary, but later in the essay he made two significant observations of a different kind: "With the imperiousness natural to all art, style absolutely refuses to avail itself of, or to be found in company with, anything that is ready made. The rule must be a leaden one, the mould made for the occasion, and broken after it has passed."[17] And he added, more specifically, that "the sentence is the unit of style, and by the cadence and music, as well as by the purport and bearing, of his sentences, the master of style must stand or fall."[18]

A long passage in the *Prose Rhythm*, thirty-six years later, in which he contrasts nineteenth- with eighteenth-century prose to the disadvantage of the former, contains some instructive comment:

Half-educated critics have a constant tendency to confuse idiom with solecism, and "bad grammar" with breaches of the rules of grammar-books which have no authority at all. They shy at words with which they are themselves unfamiliar, without considering whether these words are correctly formed, whether they supply a single designation for something that would otherwise require a cumbrous periphrasis, whether they add colour and tone to the composition, whether they increase that stock of not exact but pretty close synonyms which is the greatest treasure and glory of the English language. But these things, and many others that are commonly objected to as "slovenly," are, necessarily at least, nothing of the kind. Slovenliness is something quite different. It may be said generally to require ignorance, carelessness, and bad taste, in about equal proportions, but exercised usually in the sequence just given. The sloven does not know the good, does not care whether what he chooses is good or bad, and is inclined by his nature to the latter. But the neologist must know a little and take some pains; the parenthetical writer must be thoughtful, and anxious to express his full thought. Even slang need not be slovenly if it is employed, not out of slothful complaisance, but to give force, colour, and idiosyncrasy. True slovenliness has myriad forms; but it may generally be traced to a habit of writing, not in the writer's own way, but with tags and catchwords and commonplaces picked out of the common gutter, and huddled together regardless of the principles of real (not book) grammar, of the proper sequence of thought, of the usage of the best writers, and of the general tendency and constitution of English.[19]

In the *History of Criticism* Saintsbury noted that, "for those who hate jokes and literary allusions one can only pray, 'God help them!'"[20] In the *French Novel* he wrote that "Nothing pleases *me* so much as an allusion that I understand—except one that I don't and have to hunt up."[21] And much earlier, and equally characteristic, he said in an essay on "Tom Hood": "Life would be absolutely worthless without jest, without quip, without (let it be frankly avowed) punning. . . ."[22]

His appreciation of parenthesis is obvious from such references as "the harmless necessary parenthesis, the delight of all full minds and quick wits, and the terror of the ignorant and slow . . .";[23] and, more passionately, he noted: "Parenthesis, a heavenly maid whom there have been many and great ones, from Herodotus to De Quincey, to love, but whom few have dared to praise as she deserves. It is true that she speaks chiefly to the sapient; and the insipient accordingly do not love her."[24] Priestley considered "his extraordinary use of parenthesis, clause within clause like the carven globes in the Oriental toys" to be one of the "two most characteristic features of his style"; the other was "his uncommon use of literary allusion."[25]

In effect, Saintsbury moved boldly and freely in the vast country of prose, and there is not a single objection to his practice (apart from his occasional slips) that is not equally applicable to more celebrated writers of his day. No writer is more

allusive and difficult than James Joyce, and the following observation on Saintsbury's style might readily be taken to refer to
Joyce: "He has pooled the vocabularies of the thousand writers
inside him—though he has added undeniably original words of
his own."[26] Frank Swinnerton found Saintsbury's style "full of
family jokes, jumbled allusions, and words taken from many
languages or made up on the spur of the moment."[27] A. Blyth
Webster listed a few of them: autoschediastic, concionatory,
ephectic, estesian, indagation, irreption, Nephelococcygia, pedan-
ticulism, resipisence, perstringes, stramineous, to-deled, tritical.[28]
An elderly, somewhat exasperated but close reader of *The Peace
of the Augustans* noted most of Saintsbury's odd words and coin-
ages in the margins of that book, at one point exclaiming:
"Please, Professor, what is 'guai'?"

G. S. Fraser, on the whole favorable to Saintsbury, found
that his "personality, though it comes over strongly, comes over
largely through an old-fashioned formality and reserve." And
he said of the style itself: "Saintsbury . . . seems to write sometimes as if he had been set down in the British Museum with
eternity before him. Thus his style, with its long, loose, out-
stretching sentences, is parasitic on the literature it deals with;
in its way it is lively, but its life is less in its own rhythms than
in the quotations embedded in it, or in its appeal to the reader's
alertness to spot an oblique allusion."[29] Swinnerton declared that
Saintsbury "wrote histories of literature with the slipshod reck-
lessness of a letter home."[30] Webster himself, his chief memorial-
ist, was cautious about Saintsbury's prose. "He was faithful," he
said, "to that whimsical working style, with its Gautier-like eccentricities; which bristles with offences; but is friendly and un-
feigned and makes us fond of him."[31] And Helen Waddell wrote:

Saintsbury, said his critics, "writ no language." It was one of the many
contradictions in him—contradictions that made his very existence extremely delightful to his friends—that he whose main preoccupation
was form in verse or prose, and whose first essay, *Baudelaire,* preached
his lifelong and unpopular doctrine of style before subject, should himself write like the scour of a river in spate, allusion tumbling on allusion, parenthesis rammed within parenthesis, reckless to reject the
straws and faggots that his headlong thought swept up on its course.

But this very unselfconsciousness, this possession of the man by the subject, had its rewards. The range of his style is enormous.[32]

And she went on to give examples of his "adroit and mischievous gravity," and of the "extraordinary balance and epigraphic quality," of the "unrivalled decency," and of the "magnificence" of some of his prose. Fraser also noted a "rigid courtesy"[33] apparent in Saintsbury's manner, but Stephen Potter discovered only a "personal ghostliness."[34]

Despite either rigid courtesy (Webster had it "easy courtesy")[35] or personal ghostliness, the most frequent of all epithets applied to Saintsbury's style was *gusto*. Saintsbury had himself used the word in 1887 to characterize Hazlitt's style,[36] and again in 1904 in connection with the *Lectures on the Age of Elizabeth*. "Nowhere," he wrote, "do we find better expression of that *gusto* —that amorous quest of literary beauty and rapturous enjoyment of it—which has been noted as Hazlitt's great merit."[37] Generally *gusto* has been found to be Saintsbury's great merit also; chiefly, I believe, because it is the easiest word to use when one is uneasy about the more precise components of his style: vocabulary, allusion, conversational syntax, humor,[38] parentheses, "qualifications and sub-qualifications," periphrases, hyperbole, quotation, etc. And at the same time some critics did not think it reasonable, as the adverse ones did, to marshal the evidence of his occasional lapses and failures from his many thousands of pages.

III *Correctness Versus Personality*

The denigration of Saintsbury's style and its commonly halfhearted appreciation are based, in general, on notions of correctness: there are things that a writer should simply not do, despite the fact that almost every great writer has done them. Waywardness in prose *is* permitted to a contemporary only if he is writing experimental fiction. The critic, the historian, and the essayist are allowed no license whatever. Not one of them is to feel "free" of the language; he must learn to write like his professional and academic peers—even as bonelessly—if only he preserve correctness. With impregnable composure, "so pleasantly free from nervous airs of responsibility,"[39] Saintsbury refused; he persisted in "the voluptuous approach to literature,"[40] and he perfected "that famous style over which so many people, themselves not likely to figure in any anthologies of prose, have made merry."[41] Quiller-Couch, who thought Saintsbury worthy of representation in *The Oxford Book of English Prose,* chose, characteristically (considering *persuasion* "the first virtue of Prose"), a passage on the death of Molière from Saintsbury's introduction to A. R. Waller's translation of the Frenchman's plays.[42]

One of the best of the general descriptions of Saintsbury's manner, done much in his own fashion by a critic who shared an opinion or two with him, is by Edmund Wilson:

In his *History of English Prose Rhythm,* Saintsbury apologizes for his own prose style; but the truth is that his prose is excellent: the rhythm of his own writing never falters. He had, in fact, invented a style of much charm and a certain significance: a modern, conversational prose that carries off asides, jokes and gossip as well as all the essential data by a very strong personal rhythm, that drops its voice to interpolate footnotes without seriously retarding the current, and that, however facetious or garrulous, never fails to cover the ground and make the points. The extreme development of this style is to be seen in the *History of the French Novel* written in Saintsbury's later years and one of the most entertaining of books on literature. It is all a gigantic after-dinner talk with an old gentleman who, to his immense entertainment, has read through the whole of French fiction.

And Wilson adds that Saintsbury "found out how to manage a fine and flexible English prose on the rhythms of informal speech rather than on those of literary convention."[43]

In another essay or review in the same volume from which the above is quoted, Wilson said that, in reading *The Peace of the Augustans,* he "came at last to realize that Saintsbury, besides being a great critic and scholar, was one of the best English *writers* of his time. The spell that he can cast in his more mature work is of a kind that is not common in literary criticism; it is more like the spell of fiction or memoirs. . . ."[44] Wilson's estimate is, I believe, a just and sensitive one, and one which can be readily supported.

The excerpts which follow show Saintsbury's prose both in its gradual intensification of qualities and in its great range and variety. I begin with a passage from his first book (excepting the *Primer of French Literature*), the study of Dryden in the English Men of Letters Series (1881). This is plain, workaday prose, but with a difference: the idiom, the allusion, the ordinary word, and the freshness of material are present: "Dryden, no doubt, was not austerely virtuous. He was not one of the men who lay down a comprehensive scheme of moral, political, and intellectual conduct, and follow out that scheme, come wind, come weather. It is probable that he was quite aware of the existence and alive to the merits of cakes and ale. He was not an economical man, and he had no scruple in filling up gaps in his income with pensions and presents. But all these things were the way of his world, and he was not excessive in following it."[45]

Almost forty years later, near the end of his writing career, the full development of his characteristics is apparent in almost everything he wrote. As good an example as any can be taken from the *History of the French Novel*. In the second volume (1919), Saintsbury commented on French "naturalism"; and, having referred to its "monotonous and obligatory adultery," he provided this footnote:

I remember, in a book which I have not seen for about two-thirds of a century, Miss Martineau's *Crofton Boys*, an agreeable anecdote (for the good Harriet, when not under the influence of Radicalism, the dismal science, Anti-Christianity, or Mr. Atkinson, could tell a story very well) of a little English girl. It occurred to her one morning that she should have to wash and dress, do her hair, etc., *every day for her whole life*, and she sat down and wept bitterly. Now, if I were a little girl or boy in the French novel-world, when as I remembered that I should have, as the one, never to marry, or to commit adultery with every one who asked me; that, as the other, I must not be left five minutes alone with a married woman, without offering her the means of carrying out her and her husband's destiny; I really think I should imitate Miss Martineau's child, if I did not even go and hang myself. "Fay ce que voudras" may be rather a wide commandment. "Fay ce que dois" may require a little enlarging. But "Do what you ought not, not because you wish to do it, but because it is the proper thing to do" is not only "the limit," but beyond it. I think if I were a Frenchman of the novel-type I should hate the sight of a married woman. Stone walls would not a prison make nor iron bars a cage—so odious as this unrelieved tyranny of *concupiscentia carnis*—to order! Perhaps Wilberforce's Agathos had a tedious time of it in being always ready to resist the Dragon; but how much more wearisome would it be to be always on the *qui vive*, lest you should miss a chance of *not* resisting him![46]

The character of this prose was developed early. In 1894 Saintsbury concluded his "Preface" to Jane Austen's *Pride and Prejudice* as follows:

In the novels of the last hundred years there are vast numbers of young ladies with whom it might be a pleasure to fall in love; there are at least five with whom, as it seems to me, no man of taste and spirit can help doing so. Their names are, in chronological order, Elizabeth Bennet, Diana Vernon, Argemone Lavington, Beatrix Esmond, and Barbara Grant. I should have been most in love with Beatrix and Argemone; I should, I think, for mere occasional companionship, have preferred Diana and Barbara. But to live with and to marry, I do not know that any one of the four can come into competition with Elizabeth.[47]

In 1885 he had this to say, among other things, in the Conclusion to his *Marlborough*:

With all his weaknesses, or rather with his one great weakness, of always playing to win, Marlborough had in perhaps the greatest measure of any Englishman every great practical quality of the English character, except unflinching honesty and truth. His covetousness, though not his parsimony, can, it is to be feared, hardly be set down as altogether un-English. But the entire absence of vainglory and *forfanterie* in him, the intense businesslike energy with which he set about his work, the complete freedom from flightiness and fidgetiness with which he put the final touches on it, are all examples, on the greatest scale, of qualities on which Englishmen especially pride themselves. In Marlborough's fashion of warmaking there was emphatically no nonsense. He never wasted a man or a movement; he never executed a single manoeuvre for show; he never, either in words or deeds, indulged in the least gasconading.[48]

And thirty-two years later he wrote of Guinevere's meeting with Lancelot: "It is not, in the common and cheap misuse of the term, the most 'romantic' arrangement, but some not imperfect in lovelore have held that a woman's love is never so strong as when she is past girlhood and well approaching age, and that man's is never stronger than when he is just not a boy."[49]

[72]

These extracts should be read in connection with all other quotations from Saintsbury in this study. It will be evident, I think, that no book, no character, no episode, no subject, was ever cloistered in his mind. Everything was almost immediately pointed and involved with a variety of allusion, sometimes explicit, sometimes remote, sometimes ironic, sometimes merely humorous, always good-natured, that took it out into the world of experience, into the open air, and provided it with a kind of comparative and historical interest that is a large part of one's enjoyment of literature *as* literature. This constant breaking *through* the subject in hand, without ever losing sight of it, accounts to some extent for Saintsbury's style. He may at times have been talking to himself, but he was *talking;* and his enormous knowledge and experience, and the quickness of his mind, guaranteed that, when he met his own high standards, there were few if any to exceed his range and depth. There was in his writing nothing of that "tone of false gravity," noted by Kenneth Patchen, that is so often "mistaken for prose style."[50] And despite its elaboration, it was constantly epigrammatic:

Between a faddist and a quack there is not much more than a syllable.[51]

. . . .

It is a point of honour for one student of Shakespeare to differ with all others.[52]

. . . .

It is almost safe to say that, as is the intellect so is the interest.[53]

. . . .

A perfect autobiography would be an anticipation of the Day of Judgment.[54]

. . . .

Though ill-nature is rather monotonous, good is always surprising when it is not stupid.[55]

No doubt the growth of a poet's mind is a very interesting fact in natural history; so is the growth of a periwinkle.[56]

There is about Blake something peculiarly Adamic: he is constantly naked, but not in the least ashamed.[57]

. . . .

Never judge a critic by your agreement with his likes and dislikes.[58]

. . . .

Morpheus is unabashedly sensual; but he has some strange charm against the obscene.[59]

. . . .

Fame may be the last infirmity of noble minds; Success is but the first and last morbid appetite of the vulgar.[60]

. . . .

The Book of History is the Bible of Irony.[61]

. . . .

Oratory is, after all, the prose literature of the savage.[62]

. . . .

Nothing is more curious than the almost savage hostility that Humour excites in those who lack it.[63]

. . . .

Majorities are generally wrong, if only in their reasons for being right.[64]

. . . .

It is the nature of the fool of all times to overblame what the fools of other times have overpraised.[65]

Definitions of style are a dime a dozen. They range from the identification of style and man to the right words in the right order. Yet style remains outside the grasp of definition so long as there is expectation of an original writer in the future. But one can say with certainty that style involves the character, mind, and skill of the writer and, with equal certainty, that, if the reader enjoys the writing as well as, or even independent of, the substance, it is possible that style is present no matter how many "rules" are being violated. Certainly, the reader must be competent to judge; and he is *not*, if the breaking of "rules" laid down by pedants and pedagogues offends him, or if he is indifferent to language itself.

Obviously, Saintsbury did not generally write that "plain style" which he himself so perspicaciously celebrated in others.[66] Nor did he write a self-conscious, learned, and ornate style of a Thomas Browne, a De Quincey, a Landor, or a Pater which, as a reader, he preferred; and about which he said almost all there is to say. The origins of Saintsbury's style are, I venture, in Rabelais, Sterne, and Carlyle; but whatever tendencies were absorbed from these writers underwent a genuine change. The result is a prose free of almost all self-consciousness and guile. As friends who knew Saintsbury, and as friendly critics pointed out, it is talk, the best kind of talk: flowing, coherent, relevant, and solidly based on its substance, yet vital and mobile in its expression. Excitement is almost always present, and its presence carries the rich and allusive substance through to the reader with such ease that the reader scarcely notices the sometimes sprawling structure and the occasional lapses. Writing of Saintsbury's style, J. B. Priestley said that, "although I have found it sometimes clumsy and altogether unlovely, at others irritating and positively obscure, nevertheless I hold that there is much to be said in its favour. It suits the matter (difficult as that usually is to cope with), and it suits the man." He added that "its good qualities are . . . apt to be overlooked," and then: "To any reader at all disposed to be friendly, this style of Professor Saintsbury's soon ceases to be a trick of assembling words and becomes the fit expression of a strong and winning personality: it becomes a voice."[67] At its best, Saintsbury's style is rich, robust, and complex: and it has a variability well-suited to its subjects. In these qualities he ranks with two other modern writers of English prose, George Santayana and Norman Douglas; but Saintsbury is undoubtedly the least formal, the most conversational, of the three.

Primarily, his immense knowledge of literature *as life* and the precision of his descriptions, distinctions, and qualifications provide the foundation of his prose. Yet these qualities could result in a pseudo-scientific, authoritarian, pedagogic, or even dull manner of expression. Two or three other qualities prevent any possibility of pedantry in Saintsbury: the enormous vitality of his vocabulary and syntax; the constant, almost overwhelming, allusiveness of his mind to which he rarely denied indulgence; and the carefree delight he had in packing as much into a sentence or paragraph as the connecting words, parentheses, and qualifications would hold.

IV The "Voice"

And then there is the "voice" noted by Priestley. To give the impression of the living voice is, I submit, rather rare and, therefore, a genuine distinction of style. Much has been made, legitimately enough, of the radical differences between the written and the spoken word and, independently, of the problem of communication itself. For the majority of the peoples of the earth, almost all unequivocal communication is oral; but it is aided by gesture, movement, and even subtler means. Yet we have responded most favorably and most analytically to the written language's strong tendency to distinguish itself categorically from speech, as it does in the hands of most stylists, and to establish patterns essentially visual, with little or no implied connection with the voice.

Opportunities are not lacking to consider the movement of the language in the hands of other writers toward at least giving the impression of the living voice. There seems to be no valid reason for encouraging one tendency and for discouraging the other—for accepting, for example, the brilliant silent constructions of a Gibbon or a Pater, the deliberate artifices of a Thomas Browne or a Doughty, and for overlooking or minimizing those approaches to speech itself that are found in Swift, Hazlitt, Carlyle, and so obviously in Saintsbury himself. Unlike as each of these last four is to the others, the inner ear is conscious in each of a voice rather than of a formalized hand.

Grierson considered Saintsbury "one of the most brilliant conversationalists that I have known"[68] (he had known Saintsbury since 1896); and Augustus Muir said that "he spoke exactly as he wrote."[69] I think that this informal, almost audible quality is evident enough, however, from the printed page in all except Saintsbury's earliest prose; and it is greatly intensified beginning with the *History of Criticism*.[70]

V Fashion and Taste

The enjoyment of Saintsbury's prose is, like the enjoyment of any creative manifestation, a matter of taste and—of fashion. We accept stream-of-consciousness prose unhesitatingly these days for the delights proper to it. Why not *stream-of-thought* prose? We respond to Joyce's allusiveness, most of it extremely recondite, and are at great pains to explicate it. Saintsbury's allusions require little more than wide reading in literature itself and the pleasures of memory. His substance is usually clear even when the allusions are not understood; it simply gives added zest when we recognize what is alluded to. Is it unlawful thus to season one's prose? Is a writer to be reduced to presenting the bare bones of an idea in order not to confuse those who are dull or uninterested to begin with? I rather think not. A dull "proser" like Churton Collins may condemn both Saintsbury's scholarship and his expression of it. Later writers may echo Collins, but with some restraint. Yet no one need make himself uncomfortable over such essentially organic matters as vocabulary and syntax. No more than any man was Saintsbury infallible, either as critic or as prose writer. I have in this book deliberately cited most of the unfavorable comments on his work, comments generally directed at his style; but there were literally hundreds of favorable appraisals for each one of them.

Yet, in view of the consensus that Saintsbury was a great critic and historian of literature, we are left with an odd paradox; for almost all of those who have honored him for the quality of his pioneering work have expressed some, though sometimes slight, reservation about his style. The question as to how this unusual distinction of Saintsbury's accomplishment as historian of literature is conveyed to the reader, if not by distinguished language, is unanswered.

If it does not follow that, the greater the writer, the greater the critic (though most great writers have been at least expert critics of their own processes), it still *must* follow that, the greater the critic, the greater the writer—whatever novel form his style may take. For the discriminations, insights, perspectives, particularities, judgments, and generalizations that make a great critic *require* in him also unusual qualities in the language used to convey his ideas. Otherwise, how are they conveyed?

Saintsbury's style may, in fact, not be to everyone's taste. Yet that in itself does not disqualify it as a style finely suited to the various and complex substance. Saintsbury's balanced and reliable intuitions and elucidations are accomplished by language. The distinction of his work would not be evident if the language were poor or even commonplace. By and large, his prose rarely fails to illuminate his subject, and therein the prose has style.

CHAPTER 5

Critical Position

I Critic, Historian

USUALLY, Saintsbury's name will not, I believe, be found under the general heading of *Historian;* but the historian of literature or of aspects of it belongs there quite as certainly as does the historian of battles or of trade. Historians, it appears, only incidentally deal with works of literature in which man's best history is evident. However that may be, and despite a notable series of histories, Saintsbury is primarily encountered and considered as a critic; and, of course, critic, unqualified, means "critic of literature" and even "book-reviewer." Yet in Saintsbury's best work, as in all valid history, critic and historian cannot be separated. The histories *are* criticism, and the criticism is almost always historical: it is formulated in an immense perspective of preceding and subsequent example and practice directly experienced.[1]

This perspective is important, for it unifies and enlarges the significance of his work and makes it genuinely historical even in the confines of an essay. It is incorrect to say that the historical works "are not really histories," as George Sampson did, "but vast miscellanies lightly held together by chronology."[2] What holds them together is not chronology, which in some form or other is inescapably present in all history; it is Saintsbury's magnificent power of organization based upon criticism itself; the constant presence of a mind that relies upon experience for judgment, and describes and judges experience with unfailing honesty and independence.

II Principles of Criticism

From a viewpoint different from Sampson's, Walter Raleigh described Saintsbury's *History of Criticism* as "a prolonged assault on all systems, rules, standards, and principles."³ While this is superficial praise, it essentially misses the point. Few men have had clearer principles and sounder standards of judgment and, on the evidence of his work, have been more imaginatively systematic, than Saintsbury; and, although *a priori* "rules" of any kind for the creation or conduct of literature were offensive to him, no one had a sharper eye for the "rules" that had been followed—and the consequences of the following— in a specific work. "The immense mass of critical essays and literary histories of George Saintsbury," said George Watson, "is built upon the assumption that no critical law is ultimately worth observing through thick and thin." This he found to be —after quoting Saintsbury to the effect that biographical and anecdotic detail are harmless if "they are not allowed to shoulder out criticism altogether,"—a "sheer lack of principle."⁴ Saintsbury assuredly lacked the kind of principle Watson had in mind, yet no claim that he lacked critical principles can be supported. The modern critic simply does not recognize principles broader than, or opposed to, his own. Enclosures are the order of the day.

The key statement, sketched in ideal terms, of Saintsbury's principles of criticism, is an answer to his own question: "How do you propose to define *any* principles for your New Critic?" The reply is in the Conclusion to the *History of Criticism*:

He must read, and, as far as possible, read everything—that is the first and great commandment. If he omits one period of a literature, even one author of some real, if ever so little, importance in a period, he runs the risk of putting his view of the rest out of focus; if he fails to take at least some account of other literatures as well, his state will be nearly as perilous. Secondly, he must constantly compare books, authors, literatures indeed, to see in what each differs from each, but never in order to dislike one because it is not the other. Thirdly, he must, as far as he possibly can, divest himself of any idea of what a book *ought to be,* until he has seen what it is. In other words, and to revert to the old simile, the plate to which he exposes the object cannot be too carefully prepared and sensitized, so that it may take the exactest possible reflection: but it cannot also be too carefully protected from even the minutest line, shadow, dot, that may affect or predetermine the impression in the very slightest degree.

To carry this out is, of course, difficult; to carry it out in perfection is, no doubt, impossible.[5]

To this statement must be added, from the same work, the passage referred to above, "the old simile," explaining how to judge works of literature and art: "Expose mind and sense to them, like the plate of a camera: assist the reception of the impression by cunning lenses of comparison, and history and hypothesis; shelter it with a cabinet of remembered reading and corroborative imagination; develop it by meditation, and print it off with the light of style:—there you have, in but a coarse and half-mechanical analogy, the process itself."[6]

And then, many years later, from the first of the *Scrap Books* is the statement that "There can be no 'finality' in criticism . . ." Saintsbury wrote: "The idea of criticism as something positive and positively attainable and ascertainable, once for all—like the quotient of a sum, the conclusion of a syllogism, or the cast of a deathmask—is a mere delusion. *Criticism is the result of the reaction of the processes of one mind on the products of another,* or, to put it more popularly, it tells us how something looks to or 'strikes' somebody."[7]

These extracts indicate Saintsbury's general position, and also they account for the unintelligent manner in which he was, and is, dismissed by "scientific" critics and by those whose responses to literature, where they exist, are in the firm grasp of theory. In fact, René Wellek and Austin Warren in their *Theory of Literature* said that Saintsbury's books "are vitiated by the unclear and obsolete conceptions of meter and rhythm on which they are based, demonstrating thereby that no proper history can be written without an adequate scheme of references."[8] And, even further, they state that he "elaborately confounded psychological problems with problems of literary evaluation."[9] Worse yet, Herbert Read found Saintsbury's work "not in any real sense criticism"; and he added caustically: "His books will probably be used as manuals by several generations of undergraduates; for official education such as it is, they are perfect instruments."[10] This is really an odd gambit, for it has been, steadily since the turn of the century, the critics and scholars themselves, including Read, who have constantly used Saintsbury, both for support and confirmation—and for matters to object to or to scorn. He has been quoted, for better or for worse, by literally many more than a thousand scholars and literary men.

One aspect of Saintsbury's critical work is, then, that it is in George Watson's terms "descriptive criticism" in contrast to the two other types he distinguishes, legislative and theoretical. Description of itself, however, though it may imply judgment, does not do so necessarily. With Saintsbury, description and judgment go hand in hand; and his judgments are usually explicit and clear, and always conditioned, supplemented, and qualified by the comparative approach. This approach is at the core of all his judgments, for he emphatically believed, and always acted on the belief, that "there is no instrument more useful in the appreciation of things literary than comparison."[11]

III Limitations of Subject

Another thing held against Saintsbury as a critic was his refusal to include living writers in his histories and as subjects of his essays. This refusal, considered by Herbert Read "common in academic circles," was interpreted by him as evidence of evasiveness and timidity—as "a certain fear of life." And he thought this was "actually the explanation of Saintsbury's limitations."[12] Dorothy Richardson referred flatly to Saintsbury's "antiquated notion that the literary historian should not treat living authors."[13] Such charges brought by others besides Read and Richardson overlook or ignore Saintsbury's explicit reasons for his practice and, more seriously, the fact that for many years as a journalist and reviewer in the 1870's and 1880's he dealt with an enormous amount of contemporary literature: poetry, fiction, and other types—both French and English. He reviewed on their first appearances books by Hardy, Dobson, Hugo, Gosse, Whitman, Wilde, Swinburne, George Eliot, Henry James, Renan, Dowden, John Morley, James Thomson, Tennyson, Arthur O'Shaughnessy, Trollope, Henry Kingsley, R. H. Horne, Buchanan, and a host of forgotten writers. Reviewing current books was part of his business; and he did it well, as anyone will discover who looks through the *Academy* from 1873 to

1886. One principle in reviewing—he called it a "counsel of perfection"—was simple: "Never review a friend's book that you cannot praise, *or an unfriend's that you feel obliged to blame*."[14]

As a reviewer of current books, he defined his own practice as follows: "You may and must criticise, with as much freedom as consists with courtesy, the successive stages of the work of the living master as he submits it to your judgment by publication. But justice no less than courtesy demands that, until the work is finished, and sealed as a whole—till the *ne varietur* and *ne plus ultra* of death have been set on it—you shall abstain from a more general judgment, which can hardly be judicial, and which will have difficulty in steering between the fulsome if it be favourable and the uncivil if it be adverse."[15]

Saintsbury made a clear distinction between book-reviewing and discourse on the qualities and the history of literature. "The objection to mentioning living persons in a general history of literature, or of anything else," he wrote in 1907, "is with me most sincere and most strong."[16] Elsewhere he said: "Independently of certain perils of selection and exclusion, of proportion and of freedom of speech, I believe it will be recognised by every one who has ever attempted it, that to mix estimates of work which is done and of work which is unfinished is to the last degree unsatisfactory."[17]

When he lectured to university students, he had equally cogent reasons for avoiding the contemporary. Among them were "the difficulty of 'speaking out,' and the probable unfairness of such speaking when it is done *ex cathedra*"; the absence of a "*corpus* of more or less settled judgment" as ballast or control with respect to contemporary writers; and the fact that contemporary work is still in progress and, as such, unsatisfactory to judge. But most important of all, Saintsbury believed that it was a mistake—"almost a crime—to thrust in the personality of schoolmaster and professor between student and contemporary poet." And he added that "the commerce of new writer and young reader should be—at any rate had best be—undisturbed."[18]

Actually, once Saintsbury in his old age had become fairly well known, the deference he attracted from friends and scholars proved annoying to various schools of criticism who thought that they could "have at" the man if only he would express publicly his opinions about contemporary poets and novelists. The notion that Saintsbury did not *have* such opinions is preposterous, but he was no longer a professional reviewer. His close friends knew what he thought of this one and that, and they respected his confidence; John Purves said specifically that "in private he talked freely of his contemporaries."[19] A few such judgments can be found, explicit or implicit, in published works. For example, in 1916 he moderately praised, in a footnote, *Sinister Street,* and this, until very recently (now that Compton Mackenzie is himself a venerable figure), was taken to prove just how bad Saintsbury's judgment could be.[20] Similarly used was a letter of praise for *South Wind* which appeared in a reprint of Norman Douglas' novel.[21] Unexceptionable, however, I assume, was T. S. Eliot's dedication of his *Homage to John Dryden* to George Saintsbury;[22] but not so was Saintsbury's own and only dedication of a book, his *Letter Book,*[23] to Rudyard Kipling, for in 1922 Kipling's reputation was at low ebb.

It must be apparent from this brief summary that Saintsbury's refusal to discuss contemporary writers as either critic or lecturer, as he discussed those to whose work *finis* had been written, was based on neither ignorance of, nor isolation from, the literature of his day; it was based on sound principle. To him the critic was no jack-of-all-trades but a responsible and fully informed student of *proven* literature. Nothing is more certain than that he enjoyed as much as any man the follies and fashions, as well as the more permanent things, of his lifetime of almost three generations, but he did not choose to build a public reputation with that private enjoyment. For in the criticism, as distinguished from the reviewing, of contemporary work, one man's opinions are as good, or as bad, as another's. However confident we may be of our powers of judgment and discrimination, we are always involved, negatively or positively, in contemporary taste.

IV Emphasis on Form

A third and frequent objection to Saintsbury's practice was

his constant emphasis on form. Herbert Read accused Saintsbury of having divorced "literature and art from everything that makes it significant."[24] Others before and since have said much the same thing; they label him an "art-for-art's-sake" critic and object to an imagined separation of form and substance or of sound and sense; apparently little effort has been made to understand Saintsbury's own pronouncements on the subject. Pater himself had said, in writing of the introductory essay to *Specimens of English Prose Style,* that, if there is "a weakness in Mr. Saintsbury's view, it is perhaps in a tendency to regard style a little too independently of matter."[25] Stephen Potter went so far as to characterize Saintsbury as "the literary professor of the Aesthetic Period."[26]

As early as 1874 Saintsbury had touched on the subject of style in the *Academy:* "It is a very common error to confound a genuine love of poetry with a mere feeling of gratification at seeing thoughts and feelings which happen to be congenial to us, expressed in a manner which happens to be attractive. It is this latter which makes so many men at five-and-twenty unable to take any pleasure in Cowper and Wordsworth, and so many others at five-and-forty indignant at praise bestowed on Mr. Swinburne and Charles Baudelaire."[27] In *Corrected Impressions* (1895) there is an extended statement on sound and sense:

Readers, and I hope they are many, of Maginn's "Story Without a Tail" will remember the various reasons assigned for taking a dram, until the candid narrator avowed that he took it "because he liked a dram." It is undoubtedly natural to humanity to disguise to itself the reasons and nature of its enjoyments; but I do not know that it exhibits this possibly amiable and certainly amusing weakness more curiously or more distinctly in any matter than in the matter of poetry. Men will try to persuade themselves, or at least others, that they read poetry because it is a criticism of life, because it expresses the doubts and fears and thoughts and hopes of the time, because it is a substitute for religion, because it is a relief from serious work, because and because and because. As a matter of fact, they (that is to say those of them who like it genuinely) read it because they like it, because it communicates an experience of half-sensual, half-intellectual pleasure to them. *Why* it does this no mortal can say, any more than he can say why the other causes of his pleasures produce their effect. *How* it does, it is perhaps not quite so hard to explain; though here also we come as usual to

the bounding-wall of mystery before very long. And it is further curious to note that the same kind of prudery and want of frankness comes
in here once more. It often makes people positively angry to be told
that the greatest part, if not the whole, of the pleasure-giving appeal
of poetry lies in its sound rather than in its sense, or, to speak with
extreme exactness, lies in the manner in which the sound conveys the
sense. No "chain of extremely valuable thoughts" is poetry in itself: it
only becomes poetry when it is conveyed with those charms of language, metre, rhyme, cadence, what not, which certain persons dis-
dain.[28]

There is a further statement in his study of Dryden: "So long
as any one holds a definition of poetry which regards it wholly
or chiefly from the point of view of its subject-matter, wide differences are unavoidable. But if we hold what I venture to
think the only Catholic faith with regard to it, that it consists
not in a selection of subjects, but in a method of treatment, then
it seems to me that all difficulty vanishes."[29] And, in the *History
of the French Novel,* he says categorically: "For my part, I have
never given up the doctrine that *any* subject *may* be deprived of
its repulsiveness by the treatment of it."[30]

In the first of the *Scrap Books,* he, in considering the subject
again, expresses surprise that there should still be objection
"to the separation of Form and Matter in literature"; and he
points out "the worst and most fatal faults of criticism itself":
the need to approve the subject matter before the manner of
presentation can be accepted; and "the acceptance of the matter
because of the form, or *vice versa.*"[31] He also disassociated himself from the "degeneracies and exaggerations of practice" of
the "art-for-art's-sake" school of fifty years earlier—even while
he remained loyal to the principle. Referring to Baudelaire and
Flaubert in particular, he said: "When we praised these men
and others, when we rejoiced in them because they had followed art for art's sake, it was also, or rather at the same time,
because they had followed life for life's sake *as well.* In fact
you cannot do the first without doing the second, though you
certainly may do the second without doing the first." And he
then states:

Form *without* matter, art *without* life, are inconceivable—or conceiv-
able only like the jejune conceptions of mathematics. What we fought

against when we carried that banner was the meddling and muddling of the two, the inability to distinguish them, the stipulation that the canvas must have been bought at the proper shop, the paper manufactured at the particular mill, before people should allow themselves to enjoy the picture or the poem. And let no one suppose that this danger has passed. What was once the proper shop may have been shut up; the river may have been turned away from the old mill. But unless you train yourself to value the art and the form and the literature apart from, though by no means to the neglect of, the matter and the life, you are likely to fall, as a delightful phrase of the Articles has it, into "wretchlessness of most unclean [critical] living."[32]

In brief, substance and form are inextricably bound in any art; but the substance, clear and evident or obscure and uncertain, is, despite the celebrants of progress, nothing new. The handling of the substance—the form—is however, unique and is therefore new, if it is anything at all; and in it lies the wonder. The reader can agree or disagree with, delight in or regret the substance: the beauty, the art, and everything of moment is there in the form that the substance has been given.

Unfortunately, great subject matter is commonly handled with very little art; and trivial, even objectionable subject matter sometimes with very great art. In the first instance, what is of unquestionable importance to human dignity is being debased and should be the occasion for the severest criticism. In the second, no harm is done; the trivial and the objectionable usually make their interminable way without the favor of art; and art itself, when it happens to be present, injures no one.

V Articulate Music

Finally, though Saintsbury wrote much on the novel, on literature in general, and on criticism itself, it was always to poetry that he returned; and no book of his is free of comment on or allusion to poetry. Even when he was stating his critical position or principles, it was frequently, as is evident above, in terms of poetry. The highest function of the critic of literature was to him the discovery and the celebration of "passionate expression in articulate music,"[33] and such expression is found most frequently, most memorably, and at its greatest in poetry. "The only catholic test-question of poetry" itself, he believed, was, in a paraphrase of Hazlitt: "Is this the vivid and consummate expression, in metre, of an impression furnished by object, event, passion, imagination, fancy, or whatsoever humanity can be, do, suffer, or experience?"[34] On the language of prose and verse, it was Saintsbury's conviction that

This endlessly debated question might be settled, if critics were less litigious, by a very simple and reasonable *Concordat*. The highest poetry can be written in what is, literally speaking, the vocabulary of the most ordinary prose; but when it is—for instance, "the rest is silence," or "To-morrow and to-morrow and to-morrow," or "Put out the light,"—there is always some *additional* meaning which, in ordinary prose use, the words would not bear. And, further, this vocabulary, in the vast majority of instances, requires supplementing by words and combinations of words which would seldom or never be used in prose.[35]

Then, again, he was fully aware that "Nobody is obliged to like everything good; probably no one *can* like everything good. But, in case of disliking, the critic must be able either to give reasons (like those of Longinus in regard to the *Odyssey*) relatively, if not positively, satisfactory: or he must frankly admit that his objections are based upon something extra-literary, and that therefore, in strictness, he has no literary judgment to give."[36]

And, if we are prepared to maintain our emotional liberties and integrity, no one is going to explore the depths of John Donne or Henry James for us; no one is going to explain "scientifically" why we should love or admire one book, one writer, or one poem in preference to another; no one is going to "reveal" to us aspects of a work of art which we are not prepared to see for ourselves. That critics attempt to do any or all of these things is pretentious and unfortunate. The actual territory of useful criticism is within the boundaries of description, persuasion, and recommendation or warning. And description of what the critic sees or finds or imagines he finds in a poem, novel, or play is sheer pedantry unless it is accompanied by some account of how these observations and discoveries affect *him*, what they *mean* to him. This was Saintsbury's practice and the basis for Dover Wilson's characterization of him as "a supreme taster of poetic vintage."[37]

VI The True Critic

Also, for Saintsbury, "a true critic never holds the neat, positive, 'reduced-to-its-lowest-terms' estimate of authors, in which a criticaster delights. His view is always facetted, conditioned."[38] This accounts for his lifelong practice of giving, whether briefly in a sentence or two, or at length, a careful and rounded estimate of a man's work with precise indications of the beauties to be found and with a no less precise identification of weaknesses and faults. Unexpectedly, perhaps, this combination of black and white never produces gray; on the contrary, it results in an unusual clarity of analysis, though much fault has been found with Saintsbury when he deals thus with poets whom much later it became the fashion to overvalue.

"Dulness never will understand," he wrote,

either that those who are not dull can laugh at what they love, or that it is possible for a man to see faults, and even serious faults, in writers and writings on whom and on which, as wholes, he bestows the heartiest admiration. From the outset of his career the critic has to make up his mind to be charged with "ungenerous," or "grudging," or "not cordial" treatment of those whom he loves with a love that twenty thousand of his accusers could not by clubbing together equal, and understands with an understanding of which—not of course by their own fault but by that of Providence—they are simply incapable.[39]

The foregoing quotations provide some idea of those matters basic to "the critical approach" which were of most concern to Saintsbury—and of his unacademic and almost impromptu manner of presenting them. In summary, Saintsbury was relatively free of what Angus Wilson recently called "the censorship of educated prejudices."[40] Saintsbury left no organized, reasoned conspectus of critical principles. His convictions on the subject early became part of his equipment as a critic, and his work stands as evidence of his consistency and integrity. And, even though he repeatedly emphasized certain aspects of his method, the reader discovers not only the principles themselves but their general validity in his application of them. Saintsbury believed in the historical and comparative method and in thorough preparation. He considered criticism to be co-extensive with rhetoric. He saw little value in critical specialization, and he warned of the perversion of judgment resulting from the neglect of minorities. He thought that an understanding of the limitations of a writer or of a book was an essential aspect of appreciation. He never deviated from his belief that a work of art was distinguished from non-art by its form (its manner of presentation) and that to a critic of literature, subject matter (though far from uninteresting) is irrelevant. He considered it bad taste and bad judgment to pretend to an historical view of contemporary writers and therefore left them out of his histories. He considered it the business of the literary critic and historian to compare and to judge; to stick to literary matters and in them to fact; to judge only from firsthand experience and insofar as possible independently of fashion, convention, prevailing opinion, and his own non-literary convictions. Above all, he refused to be concerned with the manufacture or elaboration of theories of literature. "In no department of inquiry," he said in 1909, "is attention to fact and to fact only, combined of course with intelligent grasp and arrangement of fact, so rare as in literary history."[41]

Despite his reputation and the uses to which critics and scholars have put his work, Saintsbury is hardly a critic's critic. Critics themselves, though few during his lifetime could afford to ignore him, were, to the extent that they had "theories" of criticism or favorite authors to promote, obliged to disagree with him on one score or another. What chiefly bothered them, however, was Saintsbury's eclecticism, his enthusiasm, his knowledge of sources the extent of which they could never hope to equal, and his failure to engage in the increasingly popular critical sport of espousing one writer or one school of writing at the expense of another.

The many who were not professional critics—the literary essayists, scholars, preface and introduction writers, and editors —were, most of them, content with "as Professor Saintsbury says . . .," "Mr. Saintsbury happily describes . . .," "I cannot agree with Professor Saintsbury that . . .," "Saintsbury was quite right in pointing out . . .," and their endless positive and negative variations.

Saintsbury is a critic for the confirmed reader and for the livelier student. As with no other critic, one can find almost any literary work in English commented on somewhere in Saintsbury's work, a recommendation of his thoroughness as an historian; and the comment will rarely, if ever, be found commonplace. Saintsbury's notices of books and writers are always independent and frequently memorable, yet he goes no farther than to recommend reading as one of the delights of living. He puts these matters freshly in his inaugural address at Edinburgh: "In the study of literature almost everything, when rightly understood, is delightful, and the kind and variety of advantage are almost co-extensive with the province of literature itself, or, in other words, with the range of human thought and of human feeling, of human action and of human experience."[42] Earlier in the same address he had said: "For the city of literature is a true, and if not the only true yet the only uncontested, city of the world; and its municipal regulations bind Englishman and Frenchman, Greek of Athens and Scotsman of Edinburgh, with a yoke at once gratefully observed by the freeman and irresistible by the rebel."[43] And, in conclusion, he assured his audience that: "No bloom is taken off by the most careful and critical literary study: the men who have pursued it furthest and most constantly are its most untiring lovers. Here, at any rate, ignorance is not bliss, and knowledge is never disenchantment except where ignorance itself was a complete calamity."[44]

Saintsbury stimulates rather than oppresses the intelligent and the curious. And no other critic in English provides, preserves, and develops so well for his readers and students every degree of measure and perspective of which they are individually capable. What Saintsbury wrote in concluding a brilliantly conditioned passage on Johnson is equally applicable to himself: "We may freely disagree with his judgments, but we can never justly disable his judgment; and this is the real criterion of a great critic."[45]

"Here is a critic," said Edmund Wilson of Saintsbury, "who has covered the whole ground like any academic historian, yet whose account of it is not merely a chronology but a record of fastidious enjoyment." The result of Saintsbury's approach to the problem of criticism "is one of the most agreeable and most comprehensive commentaries on literature that have ever been written in English."⁴⁶

CHAPTER 6

Teacher an Last Years

I At Edinburgh

SINCE Saintsbury spent twenty years of his full maturity as a teacher, something must be said of this aspect of his activities. These were the years during which he produced three of his five major histories, despite the heavy responsibilities that he took quite seriously as professor of rhetoric and of English literature at Edinburgh: "the first Englishman who had succeeded to the heredity of Blair, Aytoun and Masson."[1] Chosen over two of his friends, William Ernest Henley and Walter Raleigh, Saintsbury became, according to Grierson, who succeeded *him,* "the most vivid personality in the Scottish universities of those years."[2]

In 1886, in his essay on John Wilson, Saintsbury, referring to Wilson's "lucrative Professorship of Moral Philosophy in the University of Edinburgh," wrote that "until he was thoroughly broken by illness, he appears to have made the very most of the not inconsiderable spare time of a Scotch professor who had once got his long series of lectures committed to paper, and had nothing to do for the rest of his life but collect bundles of pound notes at the beginning of each session." When he wrote this statement, he could not have anticipated his own professorship at Edinburgh; and it was characteristic of him that, when he came to reprint the essay in the *Collected Essays* of 1923, he added this footnote: "This was just at Wilson's time, when they actually gave a man six months' leave between election and beginning work. *I* had a fortnight; and double or treble what Wilson had to do afterwards, besides constant change of subject, but I keep this passage though (or perhaps because) I used to be chaffed about it by colleagues at Edinburgh."[3]

John Purves described Saintsbury's lectures as "a prolonged

causerie, in which he expatiated swiftly—all too swiftly for some of his hearers—on the whole course of English Literature and the principles of style and rhetoric, with occasional glances at other literatures." Purves found the lectures "an immensely stimulating commentary . . . enlivened with quips and thrusts and characteristic turns of Saintsburian humour"[4]; and, in his brief "Recollections," Purves cited a number of examples. Among the best is a comment on Landor: "all of his friends with whom he did not quarrel held him to be the most amiable of men."[5] Purves noted, too, Saintsbury's "fundamental seriousness and even melancholy," and concluded with: "My last sight of him was on a winter's night in Princes Street, near the time of his retirement, beating up against a westerly gale, an heroic figure of an antique type, *tetragono ai colpi di ventura.*"[6]

Stephen Potter observed "the growing sarcasm" of Saintsbury's examination questions and quoted as evidence: "Without remarking that the thing became a trumpet in his hands, say something relevant about Milton's Sonnets."[7] Another student, John W. Oliver, described the "class of Rhetoric and English Literature" during Saintsbury's next to last year: The thick November mist of the town, that was seeping into the room left as the "only well-lit place . . . the lecturer's desk, where two electric bulbs make a little island of light amid the encompassing darkness," illuminating "the striking face with the long, straggling grey beard." Saintsbury made him think of a familiar picture in the Scottish National Gallery, "Paracelsus, the Alchemist, Lecturing." He also noted "the determined strength of his figure; the massive power of his face," and, as also recorded by others, "the high-pitched voice" and the rapid delivery.[8]

Saintsbury's friend, George Crystal, was present at the inaugural lecture on October 16, 1895; and, in some reminiscences following Saintsbury's death, he described him affectionately as "of a truly socratic homeliness." He recalled "his burly figure" as a common sight "breasting the east wind" through Edinburgh mists. "He walked sturdily and rather stiffly," Crystal continued, "with something between a stride and a strut, always wrapped in a stout dark overcoat, muffled to the chin and topped by one of those unusual, square cut bowler hats. . . . His massive head was sunk forward between powerful shoulders, his beard projecting, and straggling a little, over the black scarf. There was a suggestion of closed fists and pugnacity about his hands, one of which always grasped an umbrella very firmly."[9] Crystal's impression of the professor can be seen transfixed in what is perhaps the most impressive of the few photographs of him, the three-quarter length study that accompanied Webster's memorial essay in the *University of Edinburgh Journal*.[10] It shows Saintsbury standing full-face, almost monumental in his great coat and hatless; his nose and brows are the most prominent features.

A woman student of his early Edinburgh days described the male students as stamping and whistling Saintsbury into the lecture room and on to the platform to the tune of "Oh, come all ye faithful," having him "absolutely in step." She found his bearing "imposing and aristocratic but not prepossessing."[11] Stephen Potter said that Saintsbury's attitude to the average student was "one of slightly sarcastic tolerance" and that, as a teacher, "he was not impressive, nor was he precise," whatever that may mean. In contrast, Elton, who knew Saintsbury well as friend and associate, described him as "a sound, enthusiastic, and successful teacher" and remarked "his humorous and glancing habit of speech . . . not always understood by the serious-minded." He quoted, from a notice in the *Scotsman* of January 30, 1933, the statement that "no department of teaching in the University was better organized or controlled by its head than that for which Saintsbury was responsible," despite the "evil tradition of rowdiness" and "the secular license of the northern student." "We learn without surprise," added Elton, "of the high regard and liking in which he was held, by his 'honours' students in particular, and by the rest in proportion as they knew him."[12]

Saintsbury's own ideas about his professional responsibilities toward his students are instructive, and they accord with and supplement his approach to critical writing. In 1914 he remarked: "For my own part I always tell my students that if, in examinations, they repeat my lecture—or book-phrases I shall 'mark them down.' All I wish to do, and all I pretend to do, is to teach them how to read."[13] After his retirement he recalled: "When I was a Professor of Literature I used to say every year in so many words, as I had previously written for more than as many years, when I was only a critic of it, 'I do not wish to teach you how to write. I wish to teach you how to read, and to tell you what there is to read'."[14] In an article in the *Athenaeum* of July 9, 1920, "On the Teaching of English," he asks: "What should be the immediate object of the teacher of English Literature?" and his reply to his own question is: "To interest the learners in reading, and to show them how to acquire and exercise such interest"; and he adds that "there is no way of producing this interest so sure, if indeed there is any other way at all, as the manifestation of his own interest by the teacher himself. It is this which makes extempore lectures so much more efficacious than written ones, and the continuous reading and commenting of texts . . . so much better than the most admirable and scholarly dissertations on things in general."[15]

One other quotation, taken from an unpublished address to young students is relevant: "The whole world of speech and thought is your province" he told them; "the accumulations of centuries and millennia are at your disposal with no prejudice to others. There is in the region of Arts a point in which it differs remarkably, and most happily, from other regions: nothing is obsolete, nothing ancient, nothing modern. Everything is an expression of the undying human mind. What has been, has been, and therefore is."[16] This statement nobly sums up Saintsbury's mind and character as teacher, critic, historian, and man.

II End of a Life

To the end of his life Saintsbury was remarkably productive. Extreme old age took its physical toll, but nothing else; his mind remained as active and acute as ever, his memory extraordinary, and his interests unabated. There was no retreat, although his physician restricted his wines and although his great library was gone. Sometime in the 1920's he had been knocked down by a taxi. His friend Elton reported that "he rose and spoke words to the cabman, who retorted that he ought to thank God for escaping with his life. 'I do thank God,' was the reply . . . 'but I damn you'."[17]

Altogether, Saintsbury's was an admirable, courageous old age spent in industrious seclusion and with few deprivations, none of them critical. Yet quite contrary impressions are to be found in otherwise reliable, as well as in unreliable, sources: impressions of poverty, of blindness, of a kind of decrepit dufferdom, even of bald-headedness—none of them with a grain of truth. "A little old man," wrote J. C. Squire of Saintsbury, attempting to describe him during his final seven or eight years, "wizened, frail, bent, rather deaf, rather blind."[18] Observations such as these gave rise to other exaggerations.

One of the most fantastic examples known to me of information invented to conform either to prejudice or ignorance can be found in *Twentieth Century Authors*, an enormous reference book in the possession of many booksellers and librarians. Its editors considered Saintsbury as Victorian, as superficial, and as having an "overwhelming interest in extraneous matters." Therefore: "At the end he was a museum-piece—a left-over old widower pottering around the Athenaeum Club, occasionally tossed a sop of reverence by critics two generations his junior, and (up to ten years before his death in London) indefatigably turning out books which in essence became more and more garrulous reminiscences of an old man who had outlived his time."[19] The editors and/or writers are entitled to their opinion; but every piece of information in that sentence is wrong; and the tone and choice of words are disgusting. Saintsbury retired to Bath in 1916, a man of seventy; he died there seventeen years later. For much of the time, after his invalid wife's death in 1924, he did not venture out.

Yet he lived and worked as industriously as ever. Subsequent to his retirement, the *Peace of the Augustans* and the two volumes of the *French Novel* were written, as well as the *Cellar-Book* and the three *Scrap Books*. The most delightful and companionable of the numerous "collections" he edited, the *Letter Book*, was published in 1922.[20] Between that year and his death, he wrote introductions or prefaces (some of considerable length) to at least twenty volumes, including such varied fare as the *Receipt Book of Mrs. Ann Blencowe,* Clemintina Black's *The Linleys of Bath,* a volume of tales by the Comte de Caylus, Walton's *Lives,* Marryat's *Jacob Faithful,* Dorothy Sayers' translation of *Tristan in Brittany,* and Dorothy Hartley's *The Old Book: A Mediaeval Anthology.*

Furthermore, he reviewed for the American *Dial* from April, 1926, through May, 1929; he commented in his liveliest manner on Poe, Erasmus, words, printing, Xenophon, technique, Blake, Boswell, Seneca, Henry Mackenzie, medieval rhetoric and poetics, Horace Walpole, Abelard and Héloise, irony, and the eighteenth century. He also wrote long introductory essays for Fitzgerald's *Omar Khayyam,* published in 1930, and for Helen Waddell's translation of *Manon Lescaut,* published in 1931—little more than a year before his death.

He was certainly no half-blind "museum-piece" whose life work was done and who was helplessly waiting for the end behind a window in the Royal Crescent. His writing was, during these years, at its idiosyncratic best; his memory and vitality, extraordinary—"in heart and wit permanently young";[21] and, though house-bound, he proved a delightful host to visitors. William Nicholson's oil-painted portrait,[22] done in 1925 and owned by Merton College, gives a memorable impression of him, seated, wearing his skull-cap and small wire spectacles, and apparently in the same suit he was wearing for the photograph that serves as frontispiece to *Prefaces and Essays.* Elton noted in the Nicholson portrait "the kindly, sagacious, and expressive eyes, under the skull-cap, and the lined features full of humane experience."[23] It is these eyes that were described by Potter as "book-quenched."[24] A friend of Squire's who visited at Bath thought Saintsbury looked to be "a mixture between the Rabelaisian and the Rabbinical."[25]

Writing to Grierson on September 26, 1927, Edmund Gosse protested that Saintsbury "is 82 (not 81), and going strong. I constantly have cheery postcards from him, which take hours to decipher but are worth it. He suffers, he says, from giddiness, which confines him entirely to the house, but his brain and pen are as efficient as ever."[26] Dorothy Margaret Stuart, who saw him frequently during his last years, described her first visit in August, 1926: "I entered the large, light, book-encumbered room looking out on the Crescent Fields, and a figure in a black skull-cap rose from behind a table by the window. It seemed to go on rising longer than the supposed short person had any right to do. As a matter of sober history, Saintsbury stood five feet eleven inches without shoes; and even his curious high-shouldered stance could not make him appear other than tall. It is strange that a disciple who visited him at Bath should have described him as 'a little old man,' and his habitat as 'a basement'." Further, in 1932 his oculist said "that his eyes 'would last his time'—and they did."[27]

Helen Waddell in her tribute, "The Man of Books," briefly summarized Saintsbury's career: "He married young: he had Prospero's island of enchanted lawn at the beginning of life instead of at the end, and all his years were transfigured by it: and he was supremely his own master." She thought that "as a letter-writer he ranks with Walpole and with Lamb," and she called his letters "quintessential." And she closed her brief essay by describing the Saintsbury she knew and honored most: "the solitary scholar who was his own best company, 'Lord not only of Joyous Gard but also of Garde Douleureuse,' reading, reading, reading through the small hours in the familiar chair with the two tall candlesticks behind it. And their light falls, not on his face, but on the open book."[28] And Rudyard Kipling, remembering back to the days of the Savile Club and the "kindness and toleration" of the friends he made there, included one whom he was to outlive: "Saintsbury, a solid rock of learning and geniality whom I revered all my days; profoundly a scholar and versed in the art of good living."[29]

Three volumes of Saintsbury's *Collected Essays and Papers* were published in 1923 and a fourth in 1924. These were a gathering of studies from his earlier books of essays, with a few additions. A little more than a year before his death, the introductions to the Oxford *Thackeray* appeared as *A Consideration of Thackeray*. Posthumously, these volumes were supplemented by four more of solid work. Elton edited a book of *Prefaces and Essays* collected from various sources, chiefly Saintsbury's introductions to the novels of Fielding, Sterne, Smollett, and Peacock and those to some single works such as Swift's *Polite Conversation; The Heptameron;* Donne's *Poems;* Jane Austen's

Pride and Prejudice; and others. A year later (1934), Cambridge University Press issued in a separate volume his study of Shakespeare from the *Cambridge History of English Literature.* In 1945 the *Memorial Volume* appeared; it contained a great deal of previously uncollected work, including further prefaces and introductions, the seventy-seventh birthday *Address* and *Reply,* and material from journals and newspapers. This volume also contained "Personal Portraits," by Elton, Grierson, John W. Oliver, and John Purves, in addition to Webster's "Biographical Memoir."

The next year an American, Huntington Cairns, edited, with a discriminating and appreciative introduction, twelve of the thirty-eight articles on French literature and the essays on French writers from the eleventh edition of *Encyclopaedia Britannica;* one hundred sixty-seven of the three hundred seventeen pages are taken up by the remarkable survey of French literature. In 1950, another collection of "Essays and Papers," *A Last Vintage,* was published. It included essays from the *Times Literary Supplement,* the *Dial,* the *Criterion,* and other sources; further introductions, prefaces, and "contributions"; and another sheaf of "personal portraits," this time by David Nichol Smith, Dorothy Margaret Stuart, and Helen Waddell.

Whatever reasons Saintsbury had for rejecting or ignoring the material collected in these posthumous volumes had nothing to do with its quality. These notes and studies—some extensive, some brief—can stand securely on an equal footing with the rest of his work. There is scarcely one of them that does not contribute sidelight and insight, that cannot be read with gratification in connection with the literature or events it discusses.

On October 23, 1922, his seventy-seventh birthday, Saintsbury was presented, at his apartment in the Royal Crescent at Bath, with an address transcribed on vellum by the great calligrapher Edward Johnston; and it was signed by hundreds of friends, former students, and strangers grateful to him for his books. The address, brought to Bath by George Crystal and by John Squire as delegates, paid tribute to the old man in memorable words, of which some at least must be quoted. "The noble art of rational enjoyment," the address said, which you have preached so steadily from a hundred texts, you have neither practised nor inculcated apart from the rigorous discipline of study. For the abstract delights of theory and system you have never greatly cared. But you have counted no labour misspent by which a student's actual acquaintance with books might be enlarged or his faculty of literary comparison increased; and your own criticism bears ample evidence of the stores of first-hand knowledge on which it is based. Some of the tasks which you have set yourself have been formidable and even heroic, but they have been conceived and carried out, like all your work, with so high-hearted an enthusiasm that no more spirited and companionable works of erudition than yours have been published in our time.

The address also spoke in behalf of former students: "On all the themes of your discourse they recall with gratitude words witty, provocative, and wise; and they count it also a piece of good fortune that you came to them not from the sheltered seclusion of the schools, but from the open arena of letters, bringing with you inspiration and experience from that wider field." And further:

Both by precept and example you have given to your juniors in literature, to many who have never seen your face, instruction and guidance for which they owe you the deepest gratitude. You have always seen Literature as the flower of a vigorous life. You have shown how an unsurpassed catholicity of taste may be united to an ardent passion of appreciation, how a zest for the small and curious may live with a recognition of and a reverence for the great. You have insisted on the importance of the minutiae of craftsmanship whilst retaining a healthy contempt for preciosity. Without moralizing you have been a moralist, whose every page has inculcated manliness, courage, and a relish of life.

The exquisite calligraphy was recognized with his usual humor by Saintsbury in his reply. He accepted the loveliness of the script "as a much needed lesson" to one whose own writing, because of a deformation of the hand, was notorious for its almost total undecipherability. And he concluded with this noble statement:

As to the details of the gracious eulogy which you and your companions have pronounced on me, I think nothing can be more appropriate than some well-known words of Dr. Johnson: "It is not for me to bandy civilities" with those who wish to do me honour. At a very early time of my life it was, as the old phrase goes, borne in upon me that I was not destined to create great literature, but that I had perhaps some faculty of appreciating it, and might even to some extent assist that appreciation in others. You and your co-signatories seem to tell me that in thus thinking I did not merely flatter myself; but I desire no greater praise.[30]

Saintsbury is easily forgiven for equating "great literature" exclusively with romance and poetry and for forgetting momentarily his own celebration of certain documents of criticism as literature. If his best work is not literature, as the histories of Gibbon and Carlyle are literature, and in its own field incomparable, one is at a loss for a rational definition of the subject. Many of his brilliant predecessors and contemporaries had put their genuine learning and scholarship into books, respected and valuable books to which duty at times compels us; but they did little more. Saintsbury injected much more than knowledge into what he wrote. He put in the whole of himself: all those aspects of a rich experience, serious and jocose, which he had gathered in, seen in its immediacy and in its permanence, judged with unfaltering discrimination, and then made a living part of anything he had to say. No writer of our time responded so truly to so much outside himself with so much within. Although we may go to his books for knowledge, wisdom and delight are also waiting for us.

CHAPTER 7

Conclusion

I T is quite true with regard to Saintsbury that, as Dorothy
Richardson wrote in 1944, "the advent of scientific techniques
and ideals of scholarship has not helped his reputation";[1] and
the neglect of Saintsbury is unfortunate. For Saintsbury had
no interest in "scientific techniques" while there were "creative
techniques" to stimulate and beguile him and he went at his
work with an extraordinary equipment of his own. His ideals
of literary scholarship were such as had proved themselves and,
since they furthered his performance and in no way hindered it,
they were "scientific" enough for him. They kept him in touch
with both literature and life, and they prevented his going off
on possibly absorbing but certainly non-literary tangents.

He cultivated his chosen garden, one which all true lovers
of literature itself inhabit, with a thoroughness, a sensitiveness,
and an enthusiasm shared by few English critics. In his old
age his phenomenal reading was too often and too readily remarked upon, and it was—and still is—insufficiently recognized
that behind the reading was an intellect. That mind shaped a
series of literary histories and volumes of essays, causeries, and
studies unequaled before or since for knowledge, insight, and
vitality of expression. As a poet said not long ago, in a broadcast: "George Saintsbury, as a person, put more diversity of
inward experience with oneness of living, together, than nearly
anyone else."[2]

He wrote, not mainly for scholars, but for an educated public
that read widely and independently; and perhaps such a public
is fast disappearing. While there are books and libraries, however, it cannot disappear altogether. And although the scholars
once read Saintsbury, they are not likely to again, regions of
learning having become incredibly specialized. It is probably

true that in general scholars are read today only by other scholars and by students required to consult "the authorities" on a given writer or subject. The scholars who read and honored Saintsbury were of a different and more liberal breed; to them, specialization was only the concentration of a broad and embracing vision of literature: Oliver Elton, Herbert Grierson, William Paton Ker, G. Gregory Smith, Donald Tovey, D. S. MacColl, Walter Raleigh, A. B. Webster, F. J. Furnivall, Walter Pollock, S. H. Butcher, F. J. Snell, T. S. Omond, C. E. Vaughan, Walter Skeat, D. Nichol Smith, and others.

Non-scholars, however, who in reading explore much beyond the contemporary, will find in Saintsbury a matchless companion, a writer whose knowledge of his subject has never seriously been in question, and whose manner or prose "style" is as close to brilliant talk—the reader keeping it from becoming monologue by his own recognitions, questions, disagreements, and glosses—as one is likely to find on the printed page.

Saintsbury did not try to tell the reader what use he could make of this or that author for his contemporary emotional needs, or to point out that certain celebrated writers were of no consequence to the all-important present. He tried to deal with the literary works of man's mind *sub specie aeternitatis*; and, by and large, he succeeded. Several generations have already responded to his estimates of individual writers, one finding them independent and brilliant; the next, academic and useless; and the next, turning to him again for the sake of what Augustus Ralli called "his unspoilt power of direct vision."[3] And Saintsbury's view of life was noble and romantic to the core; but it had a strong mixture of humor, scepticism, irony, and pessimism—a "conditional pessimism"[4] Elton called it—that kept his kaleidoscopic responses free of nonsense and pretension.

Notes and References

Chapter One

1. *A Second Scrap Book* (London, 1923), p. 132.
2. *A Last Vintage: Essays and Papers by George Saintsbury,* eds. John W. Oliver, Arthur Melville Clark, and Augustus Muir (London, 1950), p. 106. This volume includes personal portraits by David Nichol Smith, "A Centenary Tribute"; Dorothy Margaret Stuart, "The Last Years"; Helen Waddell, "The Man of Books"; and a bibliography by W. M. Parker.
3. Unless otherwise noted, information and quotations in this chapter are from *A Second Scrap Book,* pp. 1-103.
4. Louise Creighton, *Life and Letters of Mandell Creighton* (London, 1904), I, 21-25.
5. *Ibid.,* I, 23.
6. *Ibid.,* I, 24.
7. *Ibid.,* I, 29.
8. *A Scrap Book* (London, 1922), p. viii.
9. *A Second Scrap Book,* pp. 71-72. Frank Swinnerton paraphrased this as: "On leaving the University he became a sybarite schoolmaster, teaching classics for six years in Guernsey," *Background With Chorus: A Footnote to Changes in English Literary Fashion between 1901 and 1917* (London, 1956), p. 69. And Stephen Potter, on what authority I am unaware, recorded that: "For a time he taught, rather miserably, at a school in Guernsey," *The Muse in Chains: A Study in Education* (London, 1937), p. 128.
10. *Notes on a Cellar-Book* (London, 1920), pp. 13-14.
11. Evan Charteris, *The Life and Letters of Sir Edmund Gosse* (London, 1931), p. 101.
12. *Andrew Lang: A Critical Biography* (Leicester, 1946), p. 56.
13. *A Scrap Book,* p. 58.
14. *A Last Scrap Book* (London, 1924), p. 198. The *Scrap Books* will hereafter be referred to as *Scrap Book I, II,* and *III.*

15. Saintsbury's first published writing was a review of Théodore de Banville's *Idylles Prussiennes* in the *Academy* for July 1, 1873.

16. *George Saintsbury: The Memorial Volume*, eds. Augustus Muir and John W. Oliver (London, 1945), p. 35. Hereafter referred to as *Mem. Vol.* It includes personal reminiscences as follows: "George Saintsbury" by Oliver Elton; "Some Personal Memories" by Herbert Grierson; "Recollections of Saintsbury" by John Purves; "The Professor" by John W. Oliver; and "A Biographical Memoir" by A. Blyth Webster.

17. "Edgar Allan Poe," *The Dial*, LXXXIII (Dec., 1927), 463.

18. Sixth ed. with a supplementary chapter by T. B. Rudmose-Brown and a new preface by Saintsbury appeared in 1925.

19. Third ed., revised (1891), p. 5.

20. *A First Book of English Literature* (London, 1914). Reprinted 1914, 1918, 1919, 1920, 1926, and 1928.

21. *A Short History of French Literature* (Oxford, 1882), p.v. A text in the Clarendon Press series; each subsequent edition, except the 6th, was revised and corrected: 2nd ed., 1884; 3rd, 1889; 4th, 1892; 5th, 1897; 7th and last, 1918.

22. *Ibid.*, p. vii.

23. See "Preface to Fifth Edition" and Webster's account in his "Biographical Memoir," *Mem. Vol.*, pp. 37-40. Paul Bourget's review appeared in the *Academy* (Feb. 10, 1883), and Gaston Paris' in *Romania*, XII (1883), 602-5.

24. Scherer's review was in *Le Temps*, Sept., 1887. There was also an article on the 2nd ed., "Une histoire anglaise," in *Études sur la littérature contemporaine*, X (1895), 137-57.

25. Edmond Scherer, *Essays on English Literature*, trans. George Saintsbury (London, 1891).

26. *French Literature and Its Masters*, ed. Huntington Cairns (New York, 1946), p. vi.

27. *A History of Elizabethan Literature* (London, 1887), pp. viii-ix.

28. Described by C. H. Herford at the time as "extraordinarily learned, extraordinarily independent, clean as daylight, and honest to a fault," *The Bookman*, IX (March, 1896), 185.

29. *A History of Nineteenth Century Literature* (London, 1896), p. vii.

30. *A Short History of English Literature* (London, 1898), p. vi. This volume has never, I believe, been out of print. The twentieth printing is dated 1960 (London).

31. "A Centenary Tribute" by David Nichol Smith in *A Last Vintage*, p. 13.

32. *Dryden* (London, 1881), p. v.

33. Second ed. (London, 1902). A brief account of Collins' pathetic career and its successive disappointments will be found in Swinnerton's *Background With Chorus*, pp. 57-60, where it is pointed out that this flayer of his superiors was himself found remiss in his one elaborate work of scholarship, the Clarendon Press edition of Robert Greene.

34. "A Biographical Memoir," *Mem. Vol.*, p. 53.

35. *Ephemera Critica*, 2nd ed. (Westminster, 1902), pp. 101-2.

36. *A History of Criticism and Literary Taste in Europe from the Earliest Texts to the Present Day* (Edinburgh, 1900-2-4), II, 488. Hereafter referred to as *Hist. Crit.*

37. *Short History of English Literature*, p. v.

Chapter Two

1. J. B. Priestley, *Figures in Modern Literature* (London, 1924), p. 146.

2. Julian Symons, *A. J. A. Symons: His Life and Speculations* (London, 1950), p. 142.

3. *Hist. Crit.*, I, vi.

4. Oliver Elton, *George Edward Bateman Saintsbury* (London, 1933), p. 16. Hereafter referred to as *Elton: Saintsbury.*

5. *Hist. Crit.*, I, 3-4.

6. *Ibid.*, III, vi.

7. *Ibid.*, II, 576.

8. *Elton: Saintsbury*, p. 16.

9. Joel E. Spingarn, "The Origins of Modern Criticism," in *Modern Philology* (Chicago, 1903-4), I, 477.

10. Benedetto Croce, *Aesthetic As Science of Expression and General Linguistic*, trans. Douglas Ainslie, rev. ed. (New York, 1922), p. 477.

11. Dorothy Richardson, "Saintsbury and Art for Art's Sake," *PMLA*, LIX (1944), 259.

12. *Ibid.*, p. 255.

13. Cf. Wordsworth: "The Poet writes under one restriction only, namely, the necessity of giving immediate pleasure to a human Being possessed of that information which may be expected from him, not as a lawyer, a physician, a mariner, an astronomer, or a natural philosopher, but as a Man. . . . We have no sympathy but what is propagated by pleasure. . . ." Preface to 2nd ed. of *Lyrical Ballads*.

14. Webster, "Biographical Memoir," in *Mem. Vol.*, p. 55.

15. *Ibid.*

16. Elton, "George Saintsbury," in *Mem. Vol.*, p. 6.

17. *A History of English Criticism: Being the English Chapters of A History of Criticism and Literary Taste in Europe, Revised, Adapted, and Supplemented* (Edinburgh, 1911).

18. *Loci Critici: Passages Illustrative of Critical Theory and Practice from Aristotle Downwards* (Boston, 1903).

19. *Short Hist. of Eng. Lit.*, p. 709.

20. George N. Shuster, *The English Ode from Milton to Keats* (New York, 1940), p. 15.

21. S. Foster Damon, *Amy Lowell: A Chronicle with Extracts from her Correspondence* (New York, 1935), pp. 412-13. Saintsbury had neatly anticipated this kind of irritated criticism: "There is nothing which one should be slower to impute, save on the very clearest evidence, than ignorance of a subject of which the writer professes knowledge; and one should be slow, not merely on general principles of good manners, but because there is nothing which the baser kind of critic is so ready to impute." *Hist. Crit.*, II, 531.

22. (New York, 1941), p. 750.

23. *A History of English Prosody from the Twelfth Century to the Present Day* (London, 1906-8-10), I, v-vi.

24. *Ibid.*

25. *Ibid.* See an unsigned article in the *Athenaeum* (London), No. 4649 (June 6, 1919), p. 432. The writer said: "Professor Saintsbury was sowing dragon's teeth when he wrote his History of English Prosody," and: "The great merit of his 'History of Prosody' is the fact that it contains the least possible quantity of theory to the greatest possible quantity of literary appreciation."

26. *Hist. of Eng. Prosody*, I, ix.

27. *Some Recent Studies in English Prosody* (London, 1919), p. 1.

28. *Ibid.*, pp. 1-2. In reviewing M. A. Bayfield's *The Measures of the Poets: A New System of English Prosody*, Saintsbury wrote: "To me, as to the enormous majority of persons in all ages who have dealt with the subject, metre *is* rhythm, made recurrent and regulated so as to provide poetical music. No other 'metre' exists for me, and I do not argue *de non existentibus*." *Athenaeum*, No. 4673 (Nov. 28, 1919), p. 1268.

29. *Elton: Saintsbury*, p. 18. In this connection, see e. e. cummings, *Six Nonlectures* (New York, 1962), p. 68: "Nothing measurable can be alive; nothing which is not alive can be art; nothing which cannot be art is true: and everything untrue doesn't matter a very good God damn. . . ."

30. *Scrap Book* III, 198, note.

31. *A History of English Prose Rhythm* (London, 1912), p. ix.

32. *Ibid.* (reprinted 1922 with "Note to Second Impression, on Quantity and Some Other Things"), p. vii.

33. *Ibid.*, pp. viii-ix.

34. Oliver Elton, *A Sheaf of Papers* (London, 1922), p. 130.

35. *Ibid.*, p. 132.

36. *Ibid.*, p. 136.

37. Herbert Read, *English Prose Style* (New York, 1952), p. 58.

38. Read, *English Prose Style* (New York, 1928), p. 65. This passage is omitted from the 1952 ed.

39. *Some Recent Studies in English Prosody*, p. 6.

40. *Prose Rhythm*, p. 450.

41. *Ibid.*, p. 443.

42. London, 1916. Hereafter referred to as *P. of A.*

43. *P. of A.*, p. vii.

44. Grierson, "Introduction," *P. of A.*, Oxford World's Classics series (London, 1946), p. xiii.

45. *Ibid.*, p. v. "One of its special glories in its own eyes": its poetry.

46. *Ibid.*

47. *Ibid.*

48. *Ibid.*, p. vii.

49. *Last Vintage*, p. 36.

50. "Biographical Memoir," *Mem. Vol.*, pp. 58-59.

51. *Figures in Modern Literature*, p. 156.

52. Robert Lynd, *The Art of Letters* (London, 1920), p. 172.

53. *Ibid.*, p. 173.

54. *Ibid.*, p. 174.

55. *Ibid.*, p. 178.

56. *Elton: Saintsbury*, p. 20.

57. Frank Swinnerton's phrase, *Background with Chorus* (London, 1956), p. 71.

58. *P. of A.*, pp. 201-2.

59. *Ibid.*, p. 157.

60. *Ibid.*, p. 339.

61. *Ibid.*, p. 142, note.

62. *Ibid.*. pp. 13-14.

63. Webster, "Biographical Memoir," *Mem. Vol.* p. 59.

64. *A History of the French Novel (To the Close of the 19th Century)* (London, 1917-19), I, v-vi.

65. Priestley, *Figures in Modern Literature*, p. 147.

66. *Sheaf of Papers*, p. 79.

67. *French Novel*, II, 463.

68. *Ibid.*, II, 461-62.

69. *Studies in Ten Literatures* (New York, 1925), p. 14.
70. *The English Novel* (London, 1913), p. 275.
71. *Ibid.*, p. 200.

Chapter Three

1. *Tristan in Brittany,* trans. Dorothy Leigh Sayers; Introduction by George Saintsbury (New York, 1929), p. xxvi.
2. "I have confessed more than once that this [technical scholarship] never was my strong point, and so much of it as I ever had is no doubt stale stuff now." *Scrap Book III,* 126.
3. *The Dramatic Works of John Dryden, with a Life of the Author by Sir Walter Scott,* ed. George Saintsbury (Edinburgh, 1882), II, 6-7.
4. *Dryden: A Study of His Poetry,* 3rd ed. (New York, 1946), p. 240.
5. *The Poems of John Dryden,* ed. John Sargeaunt (London, 1913), p. xi.
6. *Dryden: The Dramatic Works,* ed. Montague Summers (London, 1931-32), I, x.
7. *Ibid.,* I, ix-x.
8. *Ibid.,* I, xcv, note 5. Saintsbury had earlier, in 1902, described the "Heroic Poem" as "a Boojum—that is to say, it was not only something undiscoverable, but something which had a malign and, indeed, destructive influence on those who thought they had discovered it." And, in a most characteristic footnote to this dangerous variety of snark, he adds: "This Boojum, I fear, will disturb some of my friends. But I put him under the protection of the Powder of Pimperlimpimp, and of the Equinoctials of Queubus." *Hist. Crit.,* II, 368.
9. *Literature and Wine: Recollections of a Saintsbury Student* (London, 1945), p. 5. A privately printed pamphlet.
10. *Minor Poets of the Caroline Period* (Oxford, 1905-6-21), I, iii.
11. *The Poetical Works of Robert Herrick,* ed. George Saintsbury (London, 1893), I, vi-vii.
12. *Caroline Poets,* I, 313.
13. *Ibid.,* I, xvi.
14. *Ibid.,* III, v.
15. John Drinkwater, "Preface" to *The Poems of Sidney Godolphin,* ed. William Dighton (Oxford, 1931), p. v.
16. *Concepts of Criticism* (New Haven, 1963), p. 71. Poe chose the epigraph at the head of his story of "William Wilson" from that "poetical" poem (of almost three hundred pages in Saintsbury's Vol. I), *Pharonnida,* by William Chamberlayne. Another of his tales, "The

Assignation," is headed by a quotation from Henry King, whose poems are in Vol. III.

17. *The Muse in Council* (New York, 1925), p. 199.
18. *Books and Persons* (London, 1917), p. 42.
19. *Ibid.*, p. 43.
20. *The Georgian Literary Scene*, 6th ed. (London, 1950), p. 191.
21. Edith Batho and Bonamy Dobrée, *The Victorians and After* (New York, 1938), p. 344.
22. In the Fur and Feather Series ed. by Alfred E. T. Watson: *The Partridge* (London, 1893); *The Grouse* (London, 1894).
23. For a review of the *Cellar-Book*, see "Wine and Mr. Saintsbury," in *Books on the Table* (London, 1921), by Edmund Gosse, pp. 193-98. The *Cellar-Book* is still in print, the most recent edition being a reissue with a preface by Andrew Graham (London, 1963).
24. Elton, "George Saintsbury," *Mem. Vol.*, p. 1.
25. *Masters and Men* (London, 1923), p. 179.
26. "Note to Third Edition" (1920), p. xxiv.
27. *Figures in Modern Literature*, p. 156.
28. Elton, "George Saintsbury," *Mem. Vol.*, p. 2.
29. *Ibid.*, p. 1. Small private presses in England and America would do well to look into Saintsbury's *Scrap Books* for excellent material. Any one of the "Little Necrologies," the series on "Oxford Sixty Years Since," on "Le Temps Jadis," and any of the "Twin Cameos," would, if the allusion and quotation were interestingly annotated, make valuable and unusual independent books quite deserving of having craftsmanship and affection spent on them.

Much of his earlier unreprinted book-reviewing for the *Academy* and elsewhere also deserves examination: there is material here for an excellent volume. And, more than anything else, as an introduction to students and readers of Saintsbury at his best as an observer and critic of men and books, there is, I believe, occasion for a compendious anthology of passages from the whole range of his work.

30. *Cellar-Book*, p. 153.
31. *Scrap Book II*, 86.

Chapter Four

1. *Hist. Crit.*, I, 14.
2. *Ibid.*, II, 520.
3. *The Letters of Gerard Manley Hopkins to Robert Bridges*, ed. Claude Colleer Abbott (London, 1935), pp. 128-29.
4. *The Letters of Oscar Wilde*, ed. Rupert Hart-Davis (New York,

1962), p. 184. Wilde's letter was originally published over the pseudonym "Oxoniensis" in the *Pall Mall Gazette,* Jan. 15, 1886.

5. *Ephemera Critica,* p. 109.

6. In *A. J. A. Symons* by Julian Symons, p. 142.

7. *Background with Chorus,* p. 71.

8. *Cities and Men* (New York, 1927), p. 44.

9. *Books and Persons,* p. 269.

10. *Letters,* p. 184.

11. Walter Pater, *Essays from the "Guardian"* (London, 1896), p. 4. In a small handbook on Victorian Literature (New York, 1897), pp. 174-75, Clement Shorter included a most favorable paragraph on Saintsbury, but he also made the following curious statements: "His acquaintance with English literature in the seventeenth century has . . . considerably vitiated his style. It is not easy to tolerate the phraseology of the seventeenth century in modern books. This defect of style is regrettably noticeable in two volumes of literary history which Professor Saintsbury has published, one dealing with the seventeenth century and the other with the nineteenth century."

The *History of Nineteenth Century Literature* had been published the year before the above was written. What the seventeenth-century volume was, it is impossible to tell. And what, in any case, is "seventeenth century phraseology?" Whose? John Dryden's? Thomas Browne's?

12. From "Note" to *Prefaces and Essays by the late George Saintsbury,* ed. Oliver Elton (London, 1933), p. xii.

13. *Life and Literature* (New York, 1917), p. 94.

14. *The Concise Cambridge History of English Literature* (New York, 1941), p. 849.

15. F. L. Lucas, *Style* (London, 1955), p. 87. Saintsbury's sentence is from *P. of A.,* World's Classics reprint (London, 1946), p. 302

16. *Collected Essays and Papers,* III, 64.

17. *Ibid.,* III, 70.

18. *Ibid.,* III, 84.

19. *Prose Rhythm,* pp. 350-51.

20. *Hist. Crit.,* II, viii.

21. *French Novel,* II, 380, note.

22. *Collected Essays and Papers,* II, 148.

23. *Hist. Crit.,* I, 178.

24. *Ibid.,* I, 296. The parenthetical subtleties and amusements of Saintsbury's style were objected to long before the big histories began to appear. Arthur Waugh, in an article "Professor George Saintsbury," in the *Bookman,* X, 59 (August 1896), 135-36, was on the whole favorable: "the soundest, most authoritative, and most just critic among

our contemporaries." He added, however, that "his literary style (there is no denying it) is neither harmonious nor inviting. It is dry, arid indeed, disdaining charm and ornament, and occasionally involving itself in parentheses with such an intricacy that it becomes almost unintelligible."

25. *Figures in Modern Literature,* pp. 161-62.

26. Stephen Potter, *Muse in Chains* (London, 1937), p. 135, note.

27. *Background with Chorus,* pp. 70-71.

28. "Biographical Memoir," *Mem. Vol.,* p. 62.

29. George Sutherland Fraser, *The Modern Writer and His World* (London, 1953), p. 294.

30. *Background with Chorus,* pp. 70-71.

31. "Biographical Memoir," *Mem. Vol.,* p. 62.

32. "The Man of Books," *Last Vintage,* p. 25.

33. *Modern Writer and His World,* p. 294.

34. *Muse in Chains,* p. 135.

35. "Biographical Memoir," *Mem. Vol.,* p. 39.

36. *Collected Essays and Papers,* I, 124.

37. *Hist. Crit.,* III, 257.

38. Saintsbury's humor cannot readily be isolated from its contexts. In his later work it is pervasive and can best be defined as *good* humor, with a mixture of irony, verbal wit, melancholy, and exuberance. "The *great* English humourists, I take it," he wrote, "are Shakespeare, Swift, Fielding, Thackeray, and Carlyle." *Prefaces and Essays,* p. 148. I suppose that nowadays few would agree with him.

39. William Watson, *Excursions in Criticism* (London, 1893), p. 84. Of course there were others contemporary with Saintsbury and later, who persisted on their idiosyncratic way stylistically, notably the American critics Edmund Wilson and Edgar Stoll, and in England, H. W. Fowler and Robert Bridges.

40. Swinnerton, *Background with Chorus,* p. 71.

41. Priestley, *Figures in Modern Literature,* p. 161.

42. *The Oxford Book of English Prose,* ed. Arthur Quiller-Couch (Oxford, 1925), pp. 910-11.

43. Edmund Wilson, *Classics and Commercials* (New York, 1950), pp. 307-8.

44. *Ibid.,* pp. 366-67.

45. *Dryden,* p. 187.

46. *French Novel,* II, 505, note.

47. *Prefaces and Essays,* pp. 208-9.

48. *Marlborough* (London, 1885), pp. 210-11.

49. *French Novel,* I, 51.

50. Kenneth Patchen, *The Journal of Albion Moonlight* (New York,

1961), p. 219. Currently, V. S. Pritchett, like many before him, cannot believe that Saintsbury could possibly have "read the whole of English literature, and no pretence about it," without concluding that for him "perhaps literature was a total refuge from life." With no "perhaps," he adds: "Life was an uncouth interruption of literature and did not become interesting until it was written." Pritchett is, in effect, voicing the old lament that Saintsbury did not deal with the non-literary aspects of literature, with the *why* rather than the *what;* and making the unwarranted suggestion—for which there is no shred of evidence—that the *why* did not interest him. He goes so far as to say that "mystical imagination means little to him"—a statement contradicted by almost every page of the histories. *New Statesman* (April 19, 1963).

Apart from this, no rational human being escapes life and the irrational escape it only in part. The notion that living requires certain kinds of act, running for political office, fighting, having TB, playing baseball, minding other people's business, or selling insurance, is humbug. The contemplative man *lives* quite as much as the warrior.

51. *Collected Essays and Papers,* I, 277, note.

52. *Ibid.,* I, 124.

53. *P. of A.,* p. 348.

54. *Ibid.,* p. 181.

55. *Ibid.,* p. 56.

56. From a review of the *Poetical Works* of Robert Buchanan, the *Academy,* V (June 6, 1874), 625.

57. From a review of W. M. Rossetti's *Poetical Works of William Blake,* the *Academy,* VI (Dec. 5, 1874), 601.

58. *Hist. Crit.,* III, 644. This, and "in literature at least, a good thing is not made bad by a better," *P. of A.,* p. 149, are perhaps the two most important and the two most generally ignored, of Saintsbury's critical principles.

59. *The Earlier Renaissance* (Edinburgh, 1901), p. 134. Vol. V in *Periods of European Literature,* ed. by Saintsbury.

60. *History of English Criticism,* p. 493.

61. *Mem. Vol.,* p. 120.

62. *Hist. Crit.,* I, 203.

63. *The Book of the Queen's Dolls' House Library,* ed. E. V. Lucas (London, 1924), p. 308.

64. *Ibid.,* p. 308.

65. *French Novel,* II, 368. Here are several of Saintsbury's epigrammatic dismissals: "Fulgentius would appear to have given the reins, not exactly to the steed, but to the ass, of his fancy, in reference to the Mantuan." *Hist. Crit.,* I, 393. "It is among the few and peculiar laurels of the Abbé D'Aubignac to have failed in more kinds of litera-

ture than most men try." *Hist. Crit.*, II, 309. "Negligible as an authority, Brown perhaps deserves to rank as a symptom." *Hist. Crit.*, II, 477.

66. "It was a curious mistake of the late Mr. Pater, in a quite honorific reference to me, to imply that I preferred the plain style—a mistake all the more curious that he knew and acknowledged (and was almost unduly grateful for) my admiration of his own. I like both forms: but for style—putting meaning out of the question—I would rather read Browne than Swift, and Lamennais than Fénelon." *French Novel*, II, 205.

67. *Figures in Modern Literature*, pp. 163-64.

68. "Some Personal Memories," *Mem. Vol.* p. 9.

69. *Literature and Wine* (London, 1945), p. 5.

70. William K. Wimsatt, Jr., and Cleanth Brooks, writing their own history of criticism, referred in an odd, not unjust, and quite unconversational phrase to "the Saintsburyan gigantically conversational range." *Literary Criticism: A Short History* (New York, 1962), p. viii.

Chapter Five

1. George Watson touched on the need "to reconcile the functions of critic and historian, so oddly divorced in the years between the two world wars," and pointed out that "it was only by an historical accident that literary critic and literary historian were ever set at odds with each other." *The Literary Critics* (London, 1962), pp. 226-27.

2. *Concise Cambridge Hist. of Eng. Lit.*, p. 849.

3. Walter Raleigh, *On Writing and Writers* (New York, 1926), pp. 215-16.

4. *The Literary Critics*, p. 164. "When I speak of Homer, or Shakespeare, or any one else in letters, I mean the *book* called Homer and the *book* called Shakespeare. Squabbles about the *men* do not interest me." *Scrap Book* II, p. 282, note.

5. *Hist. Crit.*, III, 609. For a negative comment on this passage, see B. Ifor Evans, "The Limits of Literary Criticism," *Essays and Studies By Members of the English Association*, XVIII (1933).

6. *Hist. Crit.*, III, 546.

7. *Scrap Book* I, p. 26. See his discussion of Dante as a critic in *Hist. Crit.*, I, 437, where he noted, among other things, that it is "precisely, that apparently loose but really unerring mixture of general reasoning and particular observation which the critic requires, which prevents him from being ever exactly scientific, but which gives to his craft the dignity, the difficulty, the versatile charm of art."

8. Second ed. (New York, 1956), p. 250.

9. *Ibid.*, p. 167.

10. Herbert Read, *A Coat of Many Colours* (New York, 1956), p. 199.

11. *Mem. Vol.*, p. 151. A letter to *Commentary* (Feb., 1963) complained that a contributor "uses the comparative method to escape the effort of comprehension" and called it "this sterile technique of evading meaningful analysis."

12. *Coat of Many Colours*, p. 201.

13. "Saintsbury and Art for Art's Sake," *PMLA*, LIX (1944), 256.

14. *Mem. Vol.*, p. 195. Also: "I had not long passed my novitiate when I came to the conclusion, from which I have never since varied, that one should decline to review the work of any one with whom one has cause of quarrel or dislike, unless one can give it thorough praise on its own merits. If the varlet's jacket wants dusting, let some one else do it." *Scrap Book III*, p. 68, note.

15. *English Novel*, pp. 274-75.

16. *The Later Nineteenth Century*, Periods of European Literature (New York, 1907), p. xi.

17. *Nineteenth Century Literature*, p. v. "He gives you an ordnance map of the Past and leaves you to find your own way through the Present." H. V. Routh, *English Literature and Ideas in the Twentieth Century* (New York, 1950), p. 118. Routh here calls Saintsbury "a genial master of erudition tempered with common sense."

18. *Mem. Vol.*, p. 203.

19. "Recollections of Saintsbury," *Mem. Vol.*, p. 15.

20. Robert Lynd found this "one attempt to criticize contemporary fiction . . . both amusing and rather appalling." *Art of Letters*, p. 178. Saintsbury had (*P. of A.*, p. 149) remarked "the monotonous flimsiness of the average twentieth-century novel" and added a footnote to the word "average": "I must beg leave to insist upon this word. If the twentieth century can follow up *Sinister Street* as the nineteenth followed up *Waverley* and *Pride and Prejudice* exactly a hundred years before, the reproach of its first decade and a half will be more than taken away. Nor do I limit the benefit-exception to Mr. Compton Mackenzie. But the *average* is simply boring." To call this note an "attempt to criticize contemporary fiction" *is* appalling. See also Saintsbury's introduction to *Manon Lescaut* (London, 1931), p. xxxv.

21. In the Modern Library (New York, 1925).

22. No. IV of the Hogarth Essays (London, 1924). Eliot considered Saintsbury "a master of the literary history," but he took occasion in a favorable review of volume II of the *French Novel*, to go after what he believed to be Saintsbury's excessively appreciative esti-

mate of Balzac and his sadly inadequate notice of Stendhal. The *Athenaeum*, No. 4648, (May 30, 1919), 392-93.

23. *A Letter Book, Selected with an Introduction on the History and Art of Letter-Writing* (London, 1922).

24. *Coat of Many Colours*, p. 202.

25. *Essays from the "Guardian,"* p. 17.

26. *Muse in Chains*, p. 133.

27. From a review of *Poems* by William Cullen Bryant, the *Academy*, V (Jan. 24, 1874), 84.

28. *Collected Essays and Papers*, II, 199-200. Cf. "I insist, that Sense is nothing in poetry, but according to the dress she wears, & the scene she appears in." Gray to Mason, Nov. 9, 1758. *Correspondence of Thomas Gray*, ed. Paget Toynbee and Leonard Whibley (Oxford, 1935), II, 593.

29. *Dryden*, p. 189.

30. *French Novel*, II, 464.

31. *Scrap Book I*, pp. 85-86.

32. *Ibid.*, pp. 115-17. Again: "For Poetry deals first of all with form, Prose with matter; though the matter can never be a matter of entire indifference to Poetry, and the form becomes of more and more importance as we ascend from the lower to the higher prose." *Hist. Crit.*, I, 61.

33. *Hist. Crit.*, III, 533.

34. *P. of A.*, p. 100.

35. *Ibid.*, p. 10.

36. *Hist. Crit.*, III, 500.

37. *Macbeth*, ed. John Dover Wilson (Cambridge, Eng., 1947) p. xl.

38. *Hist. Crit.*, II, 200.

39. *Ibid.*, 450-51.

40. In *Commentary* (June, 1963), p. 542.

41. *Mem. Vol.*, p. 214.

42. *Ibid.*, p. 178.

43. *Ibid.*

44. *Ibid.*, p. 183.

45. *Hist. Crit.*, II, 496.

46. *The Triple Thinkers*, revised and enlarged edition (New York, 1948), p. 258.

Chapter Six

1. Purves, "Recollections of Saintsbury," *Mem. Vol.*, p. 13. Walter Raleigh was anxious to get this appointment, as his letters show. To

his mother, June 19, 1895: "I do want it—orthodox or unorthodox it is a *milieu* I understand. . . . Moreover my little family would like a larger income." To W. P. Ker, July 5, 1895: "If the Edinburgh Chair had to be fought for in a jolly-boat by Henley, Saintsbury, and myself I should be crippled by my respect for both." To John Sampson, July 27, 1895: "I saw Henley in London—a good man—his friends are fighting tooth and nail for him." *The Letters of Sir Walter Raleigh* (1879-1922), ed. Lady Raleigh, 2nd ed. enlarged (London, 1926), I, 184-86.

2. "Some Personal Memories," *Mem. Vol.*, p. 11. In *Scrap Book II*, p. 49, note, Saintsbury said that Henry Sidgwick, brother of William, "helped to promote me to the comparative Earthly Paradise of my chair at Edinburgh."

3. *Collected Essays and Papers*, I, 208.

4. "Recollections of Saintsbury," *Mem. Vol.*, p. 14.

5. *Ibid.*, p. 16.

6. "Recollections of Saintsbury," *Mem. Vol.*, p. 17. The Italian is from the *Paradiso*, XVII, 24, and was translated by H. F. Cary as "well squared to fortune's blows."

7. *Muse in Chains*, p. 131. Potter got this, evidently, from a footnote in the "Biographical Memoir" by Webster, omitted when the memoir was reprinted in the *Mem. Vol.* There it reads: "*Without* remarking that the thing became a trumpet in his hands, say something relevant about the *Sonnets*."

8. "The Professor," *Mem. Vol.*, p. 19.

9. *London Mercury*, XXVII (March, 1933), 434-41.

10. Vol. VI (Autumn, 1933), facing p. 56. The portrait also appears as frontispiece to the first separate printing of Webster's "Biographical Memoir" (Edinburgh, 1933).

11. Letter to the *Times Literary Supplement*, Nov. 17, 1945, signed "Septuagenarian."

12. *Elton: Saintsbury*, pp. 13-14. Saintsbury gave 107 lectures to a class of 170 in twenty-two weeks. See *Last Vintage*, p. 114.

13. *A First Book of English Literature*, p. vii. "I have aimed," he wrote, "at being as much as possible *understandable*, without 'writing down,' and as little as possible *quotable*." p. vi.

14. *French Novel*, II, 364.

15. Reprinted in *Mem. Vol.*, p. 192.

16. Quoted in *Elton: Saintsbury*, p. 13.

17. "George Saintsbury," *Mem. Vol.*, p. 1.

18. *London Mercury*, XXVII, No. 161 (March, 1933), p. 387.

19. Ed. Stanley J. Kunitz and Howard Haycraft (New York, 1942), pp. 1222-23.

20. "In his *Letter Book* he has been properly provocative—with a sting on every page." Maurice Hewlett, *Extemporary Essays* (London, 1922), p. 252.

21. Elton, "George Saintsbury," *Mem. Vol.*, p. 1.

22. Reproduced as plate 20 in the Penguin Modern Painters volume on *William Nicholson* (London, 1948). An excellent pen-drawn portrait by Powys Evans appeared in the *London Mercury*, XXI, 125 (March, 1930), 391.

23. "George Saintsbury," *Mem. Vol.*, p. 1.

24. *Muse in Chains*, p. 128.

25. Squire, *London Mercury*, XXVII (March, 1933).

26. Charteris, *Life and Letters*, p. 502. In *Scrap Book* II, p. 89, Saintsbury remarked his "very bad sight" and "malformation of the hand." In *Scrap Book III*, p. 312, he described the malformation as "a single-jointed thumb," and added that he was unable to typewrite "with more than one finger of one, and that the left, hand."

27. "The Last Years," *Last Vintage*, pp. 19-20.

28. "The Man of Books," *Last Vintage*, pp. 27-28.

29. *Something of Myself* (London, 1937), p. 85.

30. *Mem. Vol.*, pp. 215-18, where the *Address* and Saintsbury's *Reply* are given in full.

Chapter Seven

1. *PMLA*, LIX (1944), 243.

2. Eli Siegel in a broadcast interview over WKCR-FM, New York, April 11, 1963, and printed in *Definition 14*, June, 1963.

3. *A History of Shakespearian Criticism* (New York, 1959), II, 287.

4. "George Saintsbury," *Mem. Vol.*, p. 3.

Selected Bibliography

Primary Sources

Strictly speaking, there is no bibliography of Saintsbury's work. There are, however, four check lists: a rather premature list by W. P. James in the *English Illustrated Magazine* for Oct., 1903; a brief "selected" list, "George Saintsbury," in a series, "Bibliographies of Modern Authors," published in the *London Mercury*, Dec., 1919, with numerous incorrect dates; a much fuller but still incomplete "George Saintsbury: A Check List," by Walter Leuba in the *Book-Collector's Quarterly*, No. XII (Oct.-Dec., 1933), 43-51; and, finally, "A Saintsbury Bibliography," a fairly complete check list compiled by W. M. Parker and printed in *A Last Vintage*, pp. 244-55.

I list below, chronologically, the fifty-one publications (five of them pamphlets), which Saintsbury himself wrote. For the four hundred and fifty or more other volumes in which he had a hand as editor, anthologist, introducer, or contributor, see *A Last Vintage*.

A Primer of French Literature. Oxford: The Clarendon Press, 1880.

Dryden. London: Macmillan, 1881.

A Short History of the Life and Writings of Le Sage. Edinburgh: privately printed, 1881.

A Short History of French Literature. Oxford: The Clarendon Press, 1882.

Marlborough. London: Longmans, 1885.

A History of Elizabethan Literature. London: Macmillan, 1887.

Manchester. London: Longmans, 1887.

Essays in English Literature: 1780-1860. London: Percival, 1890.

Essays on French Novelists. London: Percival, 1891.

Miscellaneous Essays. London: Percival, 1892.

The Earl of Derby. London: Sampson Low, 1892.

Essays in English Literature: 1780-1860, Second Series. London: Dent, 1895.

Corrected Impressions. London: Heinemann, 1895.

Inaugural Address. Edinburgh: Blackwood, 1895.

A History of Nineteenth Century Literature: 1780-1895. London: Macmillan, 1896.

The Flourishing of Romance and the Rise of Allegory. Edinburgh: Blackwood, 1897.

Sir Walter Scott. Edinburgh: Oliphant, Anderson, & Ferrier, 1897.

A Short History of English Literature. London: Macmillan, 1898.

Matthew Arnold. Edinburgh: Blackwood, 1899.

A History of Criticism and Literary Taste in Europe: Vol. I. Edinburgh: Blackwood, 1900.

The Earlier Renaissance. Edinburgh: Blackwood, 1901.

A History of Criticism and Literary Taste in Europe: Vol. II. Edinburgh: Blackwood, 1902.

A History of Criticism and Literary Taste in Europe: Vol. III. Edinburgh: Blackwood, 1904.

A History of English Prosody: Vol. I. London: Macmillan, 1906.

A History of English Prosody: Vol. II. London: Macmillan, 1908.

A History of English Prosody: Vol. III. London: Macmillan, 1910.

An Historical Manual of English Prosody. London: Macmillan, 1910.

A History of English Criticism. Edinburgh: Blackwood, 1911.

A History of English Prose Rhythm. London: Macmillan, 1912.

The Historical Character of English Lyric. Oxford: O.U.P., 1912.

The English Novel. London: Dent, 1913.

A First Book of English Literature. London: Macmillan, 1914.

The Peace of the Augustans. London: Bell, 1916. Reprinted in the Oxford World's Classics series with an introduction by H. J. C. Grierson, London, 1946.

A History of the French Novel: Vol. I. London: Macmillan, 1917.

A History of the French Novel: Vol. II. London: Macmillan, 1919.

Some Recent Studies in English Prosody. Oxford: O.U.P., 1920.

Notes on a Cellar-Book. London: Macmillan, 1920.

A Scrap Book. London: Macmillan, 1922.

A Second Scrap Book. London: Macmillan, 1923.

Collected Essays and Papers: Vols. I, II, and III. London: Dent, 1923.

Collected Essays and Papers: Vol. IV. London: Dent, 1924.

A Last Scrap Book. London: Macmillan, 1924.

A Consideration of Thackeray. London: O.U.P., 1931.

Prefaces and Essays. Ed. Oliver Elton. London: Macmillan, 1933.

Shakespeare. Cambridge, Eng.: C.U.P., 1934.

A Golden Book. Privately printed, Chicago, 1937.

George Saintsbury: The Memorial Volume. Ed. John W. Oliver and

Augustus Muir. London: Methuen, 1945. Published in New York, 1947, as *A Saintsbury Miscellany: Selections from his Essays and Scrap Books.*

French Literature and Its Masters. Ed. Huntington Cairns. New York: Knopf, 1946.

A Last Vintage. Ed. John W. Oliver, Arthur Melville Clark, and Augustus Muir. London: Methuen, 1950.

Secondary Sources

ALLEN, H. WARNER. *The Saintsbury Oration.* London: 1948. Privately printed for the Saintsbury Club; a rambling tribute.

BALFOUR, LADY FRANCES. *Ne Obliviscaris: Dinna Forget.* 2 vols. London: Hodder and Stoughton, 1930. Contains numerous letters of the author to Saintsbury.

BENNETT, ARNOLD. *Books and Persons.* London: Chatto & Windus, 1917. Praise of Saintsbury on Balzac, pp. 42-43; denigration of his style, p. 269.

BODKIN, THOMAS. *The Saintsbury Oration: Saintsbury the Rhetorician.* London: 1947. Privately printed for the Saintsbury Club.

CHAPMAN, J. A. "Dr. Saintsbury's Heresy," *Papers on Shelley, Wordsworth, and Others.* London: O.U.P., 1929, pp. 103-14. The heresy is Saintsbury's statement that "the greatest part, if not the whole, of the pleasure-giving appeal of poetry . . . lies in the manner in which the sound conveys the sense."

CHARTERIS, EVAN. *The Life and Letters of Sir Edmund Gosse.* London: Heinemann, 1931. Two personal references to Saintsbury, one dating from 1877, the other from 1927.

CLARK, ALBERT C. *Prose Rhythm in English.* Oxford: The Clarendon Press, 1913. An important discourse on the *History of English Prose Rhythm,* critical of its method; an attempt to isolate native English from Latin rhythms. Clark believed that Saintsbury overstressed the principle of variety in English prose rhythm.

CLASSE, ANDRÉ. *The Rhythm of English Prose.* Oxford: Blackwell, 1939. Rhythm investigated from the phonetic viewpoint and conclusions based on readings made on a special mechanical apparatus. A serious study, representative of what Saintsbury most objected to.

COLLINS, JOHN CHURTON. "Our Literary Guides, I. A Short History of English Literature." *Ephemera Critica or Plain Truths about Current Literature.* 2nd ed., Westminster: Constable, 1902. A violent attack on Saintsbury's judgment, accuracy, and prose, unsupported by adequate evidence.

CREIGHTON, LOUISE. *Life and Letters of Mandell Creighton*. 2 vols. London: Longmans, 1904. Numerous references to and reminiscenses of Saintsbury in Vol. I.

CROCE, BENEDETTO. *Aesthetic as Science of Expression and General Linguistic*. 1st ed. 1909. Rev. ed., New York: Macmillan, 1922. Croce's remarks on Saintsbury are in the "Bibliographical Appendix," p. 477—Saintsbury is deficient in philosophy.

DAICHES, DAVID. *Critical Approaches to Literature*. Englewood Cliffs, New Jersey: Prentice-Hall, 1956. An analysis of Saintsbury's remarks on Prior from *The Peace of the Augustans*, characterizing his approach as "bio-critical" or "critical chat."

DOBSON, AUSTIN. *Old Kensington Palace*. London: O.U.P., 1926. Includes an appreciative and characteristic causerie on the Oxford *Thackeray* by one of Saintsbury's oldest friends.

ELTON, OLIVER. "English Prose Numbers." *A Sheaf of Papers*. London: Hodder & Stoughton, 1922. In general agreement with Saintsbury on the subject, "though with some reserve." An excellent supplement to the *Prose Rhythm*.

——. "George Saintsbury." *Essays and Addresses*. London: Edward Arnold, 1939, pp. 239-249. Brief appreciative essay on Saintsbury as critic and man of letters by a colleague and friend.

——. *George Edward Bateman Saintsbury: 1845-1933*. London: Humphrey Milford, 1933. From the Proceedings of the British Academy, XIX. A much fuller account of Saintsbury's life and work, including material based on personal knowledge.

FRASER, GEORGE SUTHERLAND. *The Modern Writer and His World*. New York: Criterion Books, 1953, pp. 293-95. Considers Saintsbury "the greatest of the professional critics," but with serious reservations about his prose.

GOSSE, EDMUND. "Mr. Saintsbury." *Silhouettes*. London: Heinemann, 1925, pp. 213-18. A perceptive discourse on Saintsbury's characteristics as a judge of literature, based on the *Collected Essays and Papers*.

GUEDALLA, PHILIP. "Mr. George Saintsbury." *Masters and Men*. London: Constable, 1923. A supercilious and uncalled-for series of sarcasms directed at the Saintsbury of the *Cellar-Book*.

JENNINGS, RICHARD. "Fair Comment: George Saintsbury." *The Nineteenth Century and After*, CXXXVIII (Nov., 1945), 215-16. Brief comment on the *Memorial Volume*, suggesting that Saintsbury may have read too much.

KIPLING, RUDYARD. *Something of Myself*. London: Macmillan, 1937. Personal reminiscences.

LEWISOHN, LUDWIG. "Saintsbury." *Cities and Men*, New York: Harper,

1927. Favorable comment by a writer who did not share Saintsbury's non-literary views.

LUCAS, F. L. *Style*. London: Cassell, 1955. Stylistic analyses of passages from Saintsbury and a negative note on the scansions of the *Prose Rhythm*, p. 221.

LYND, ROBERT. "Mr. Saintsbury." *The Art of Letters*. London: Fisher Unwin, 1920. A condescending, querulous, but appreciative essay-review of *The Peace of the Augustans* in which Saintsbury is found, among other things, deficient in a sense of proportion.

MACCOLL, DUGALD SUTHERLAND. "Rhythm in English Verse, Prose, and Speech." *Essays and Studies by Members of the English Association*. London: O.U.P., 1914, V, 7-50. Supports Lanier's musical law of rhythm in opposition to Saintsbury's prosody.

MAYOR, JOSEPH B. *Chapters on English Metre*. 2nd ed. revised and enlarged, Cambridge: O.U.P., 1901. See Saintsbury, *Prosody* I, vii, and III, 453.

MUIR, AUGUSTUS. *Literature and Wine: Recollections of a Saintsbury Student*. London: Privately printed for the Saintsbury Club, 1945. Muir was a student during Saintsbury's last years at Edinburgh.

OMOND, THOMAS STEWART. *English Metrists*. Oxford: O.U.P., 1921. An annotated bibliography of every prosodist of importance since 1545.

———. *A Study of Metre*. London: Grant Richards, 1903. An attempt to analyze the nature and construction of the metrical unit in English poetry on the basis of "time-periods" rather than syllables.

PATER, WALTER. "English Literature," *Essays from the "Guardian."* London: Privately printed, 1896. A favorable consideration, dating from 1886, of *Specimens of English Prose Style*, with particular reference to Saintsbury's introductory essay.

POTTER, STEPHEN. "King Saintsbury." *The Muse in Chains, A Study in Education*. London: Cape, 1937. Based on a paper read to members of the Saintsbury Society. Much, if not all, of the information (some of it misinformation) is secondhand, based on Webster, Lewisohn, and Elton. Potter calls Saintsbury "the Apostle of Taste" and "the literary professor of the Aesthetic Period" and finds him neither a creative artist nor a creative critic. Yet, on the whole, appreciative.

PRIESTLEY, J. B. "Mr. George Saintsbury." *Figures in Modern Literature*. London: Lane, 1924. An informal essay on the historian and critic, centered on his gusto.

RALEIGH, WALTER. *The Letters of Sir Walter Raleigh: 1879-1922*. Ed. Lady Raleigh. 2nd ed. enlarged, 2 vols. London: Methuen,

1926. Numerous references to Saintsbury and the source of information on the competition for the Chair at Edinburgh.

RALLI, AUGUSTUS. *A History of Shakespearian Criticism*, 2 vols., reprint. New York: Humanities Press, 1959. In Vol. II, pp. 287-92, summary of and comment on Saintsbury's *Shakespeare* and his essay, "Shakespeare and the Grand Style."

READ, HERBERT. "George Saintsbury." *A Coat of Many Colours*. New York: Horizon Press, 1956. A brief negative view, claiming that Saintsbury avoided the essential function of the critic.

SHAPIRO, KARL. *Essay on Rime*. New York: Reynal & Hitchcock, 1945. In decasyllables, the first of its three sections deals with prosodists, with Saintsbury, p. 11.

——. *English Prosody and Modern Poetry*. Baltimore: Johns Hopkins Press, 1947. Reprinted from *A Journal of English Literary History*, June, 1947. Discusses Saintsbury's *History of Prosody* and considers "his deliberate avoidance of theory . . . a pretty serious affair." Favors Lanier and his followers.

SMITH, DAVID NICHOL. "George Edward Bateman Saintsbury." *DNB*, 5th Supplement, 1931-40. London: O.U.P., 1949, pp. 775-77. Chief source, apart from Webster, of biographical information.

SQUIRE, JOHN. *The Honeysuckle and the Bee*. London: Heinemann, 1937. Casual personal reminiscences and exaggerated impressions, pp. 139-43.

SUTHERLAND, JAMES R. *The English Critics*. London: H. K. Lewis, 1952. Inaugural lecture delivered at University College, London. The four outstanding critics dealt with as in the main stream of English criticism are Dryden, Johnson, Hazlitt, and Saintsbury.

SWINNERTON, FRANK. "George Saintsbury." *A London Bookman*. London: Secker, 1928. Rather caustic brief tribute on Saintsbury's eightieth birthday.

——. *Background with Chorus*. London: Hutchinson, 1956. Appreciative notes on the man and critic, pp. 67-71.

——. "George Saintsbury." *Authors I Never Met*. London: Allen & Unwin, 1956, pp. 44-50. Brief, pleasant, and inconsequential essay, mainly on Saintsbury's reading and style.

WATSON, WILLIAM. "Critics and Their Craft." *Excursions in Criticism*. London: Elkin Mathews, 1893. Informal comment on Saintsbury's style, a review of *Essays in English Literature*.

WEBSTER, A. BLYTH. "George Saintsbury," *University of Edinburgh Journal*, VI (Autumn, 1933), 30-72. Published separately as a bound volume (Edinburgh: Oliver & Boyd, 1933), and in 1945 included in the *Memorial Volume*. The chief independent source of biographical and bibliographical material and an excellent evaluation of the man and his work.

WELLEK, RENÉ. *A History of Modern Criticism: 1750-1950. The Later Nineteenth Century.* New Haven: Yale University Press, 1965. An excellent account of Saintsbury as critic and historian, appreciative, but with emphasis on his limitations, pp. 416-28.

WILSON, EDMUND. *The Triple Thinkers.* Revised and enlarged ed. New York: O.U.P., 1948. Paragraph on Saintsbury's work as example of non-historical criticism, p. 258, and on the need for comparative estimates of the kinds provided by Saintsbury and T. S. Eliot, p. 267.

——. "George Saintsbury's Centenary," "George Saintsbury: Gourmet and Glutton." *Classics and Commercials.* New York: Farrar, Straus, 1950. By far the most perceptive comments on Saintsbury's mature style.

Index